CAKES
from around the world

JULIE DUFF

Grub Street • London

With love and thanks to my husband Malcolm and daughter Sian.

To Kate who loves cakes as much as I do.

To Sally and Claire whose hard work and sense of fun ensures that not only are cakes baked on time but with laughter and humour.

To Robert 'Mr Grumpy' who brings our eggs each week and ensures we continue smiling as we bake.

To Michelle, a wonderful photographer, who came to our home with Anne, to photograph our cakes with her usual skill and patience.

Finally to Anne at Grub Street for giving me another wonderful opportunity to write about my favourite subject – CAKES.

This edition published in 2009 by
Grub Street
4 Rainham Close, London, SW11 6SS
Email: food@grubstreet.co.uk
www.grubstreet.co.uk

Text copyright © Julie Duff 2007, 2009
Copyright this edition © Grub Street 2009
Photography by Michelle Garrett
Design and jacket design by Lizzie Ballantyne

A CIP catalogue record for this book is available from the British Library

Paperback edition ISBN 978-1-906502-44-7
Hardback edition ISBN 978-1-904943-76-1

Printed and bound in India

CONTENTS

INTRODUCTION

When I was writing my first book, *Cakes Regional and Traditional*, I had little difficulty in deciding which cakes to include as I was already familiar with so many of them. However when I was offered the wonderful opportunity of writing this book on world cakes, I somewhat arrogantly thought I already knew a great deal about them but I was mistaken. Certainly I knew about quite a number, but I quickly realised that such knowledge was limited – there are a lot of cakes in the world. What a challenge this turned out to be and how quickly I became totally engrossed in the subject.

Probably the most important thing I had to avoid was setting down a list of cakes similar to those from my own country or from areas of the world using very similar ingredients, kitchen utensils and methods. I realised immediately I had to remain unbiased and not to disregard any recipes, just because I did not recognise them as cakes, but to see them as exciting variations.

Another important realisation was to accept that some areas of the world simply did not bake cakes or had so few that they remained well-hidden – Thailand being a very good example. Once I had accepted this fact, I had no problem in becoming totally addicted to all the wonderful cakes which say so much about their country of origin and the people who prepare them.

When not actually baking cakes, I found myself completely obsessed with searching for information or pictures, which could give me a clue, any clue, about which cakes were baked in a particular area of the world. Recipes are almost always dependent on and influenced by the cereals, fruits and even the vegetables grown in a country.

It was also really important to consider what cooking facilities might be available – how food on the whole would be prepared in the home. The many different shapes and sizes of cakes were often regulated by where in the world they were baked and served; some countries preferring a large cake to slice, others almost always baking smaller delicacies.

There are many angles to explore and it is important to remember that cakes have a history going back generations and are often baked for special festive occasions such as Christmas, examples being Scandinavian cakes, often made from a yeast dough, totally devoid of complicated ingredients or elaborate decorations, such as the Saint Lucia Christmas Bread and the Christmas Stollen.

Many cakes also have wonderful stories attached to them. How I enjoyed the story of the cake-eating ghost or the bride married in a dress made from 1,500 cream puffs – she was marrying a baker – proof surely of why it was not difficult to become engrossed in the subject.

I always have to smile when reading a recipe which has a history of being fought over, sometimes for centuries, each claimant coming up with the 'perfect' story to back his or her claims, the bakers of the Sachertorte being a classic example, each and every recipe claiming to be 'the original'.

Another aspect of cakes is that sometimes the very name can tell a story, the Pennsylvanian Dutch Apple Cake linking the Dutch settlers – who having taken recipes with them – established their new lives in the United States of America.

The Patagonian Apple Cake is another such cake, baked by Welsh settlers in South America, but now baked regularly in Wales and appearing in Welsh recipe books, brought back by families returning to their homeland.

Somehow all these features of cake making serve to emphasize the pleasures of home baking which can never be surpassed; gathering the ingredients, preparing the cake mix and the miracle of the transformation of the raw ingredients into an aromatic delight.

Sadly it is simply not possible to include all the cakes in the world in one book, so I have tried to include as many of the most interesting as possible, together with details and stories about their history and the area of the world in which they are baked. So I do hope that you will enjoy trying as many recipes as possible while envisaging the setting in which they would be created in their home lands.

JULIE DUFF

ESSENTIAL INFORMATION

SPICES

Allspice *Pimenta dioica:* Also known as Jamaican Pepper, the spice is rather pungent, smelling of cloves, cinnamon and nutmeg. Widely used in its ground form at Christmas time, in cakes, puddings, mincemeats and mulled wine.

The Allspice tree is a member of the Myrtle family and grows to about 35 feet in height. It grows best in the West Indies or South America, the Allspice 'orchards' being famed for the aromatic scent that fills the air, the white flowers turning into the green berries, which become purple as they ripen. Later during drying they lose their purple sheen and form the characteristic rather dull brown appearance.

Allspice is also said to have preserving powers and was widely used during the 17th century to preserve meat and fish, particularly for travellers.

Anise *Pimpinella anisum:* I first encountered the little green anise seeds in a Spanish cake recipe, for *Pestinos.* A member of the parsley family, it is widely grown throughout the Middle East, South America and in parts of Russia, often growing wild.

When ground the seeds have the delicate but distinctive aroma and flavour of liquorice, but when crushed, the oil gives everything away with the heady smell of aniseed.

Often used in homeopathic medicines, anise is recommended for relieving headaches by applying the oil to your temples.

Caraway *Carum carvi:* Caraway is one of the world's oldest spices as shown by its popularity in cakes throughout the centuries, indeed in the 16th century there was hardly a cake or bread which did not include this most pungent of spice.

Not unlike aniseed in flavour, caraway bears a resemblance to a large parsley plant, being about two feet in height with the seeds forming in the large cream flower heads.

Probably the most famous cake was the Caraway Seed Cake, an old fashioned cake which, as with most of our caraway recipes, has lost popularity, but in moderation this is an interesting spice, still very widely used in Europe.

Cardamom *Ellettaria cardamomum:* Originating from India and Ceylon, cardamom is a wonderfully warm spice, fragrant and with an almost citrus flavour. The whole pods each contain 20 or so little black seeds, which can be added to cakes, the flavour intensifying if they are crushed a little before using.

Ground cardamom is made from the seeds and enjoys considerable popularity in Scandinavia, particularly Denmark where it is considered an almost essential addition to Danish pastries.

Cinnamon *Cinnamomum zeylanicum:* One of the most evocative of winter spices, bringing to mind mulled wine and the scent of Christmas festivities. In the Bible there are many references in the Old Testament, which illustrates how very precious this spice was even before the birth of Christ.

Coming from an evergreen tree of the Laurel family, the slim new branches are peeled and the bark rolled by hand to form the cinnamon quills with which we are so familiar. They are dried in the warm sunshine and it is a delight to imagine the aroma which surrounds thousands of quills drying outdoors in the summer.

Used in cakes, puddings, mulled wines, punches and indeed many other culinary treats, cinnamon can also be purchased ground, making it easily added to cakes. It is in fact very difficult to grind cinnamon at home as the quills do not break evenly, tending to splinter.

Cloves *Eugenia caryophyllus:* Reminiscent of childhood, apple pies and apple cake never seemed quite right without the addition of a small amount of clove. In fact writing about them here takes my mind straight to the evocative smell of my mother's Sunday apple pies. However it is important to use them with care as they can be overpowering.

Grown mainly on the islands of the East African coast, Zanzibar and Pemba being the world's largest producers, the cloves are the unopened flower buds of the tree, which are hand picked before the little buds have the chance to form into flowers. The trees are about 30 to 40 feet so this is quite a task, and although I have never had the fortune to be near to one of them, I understand that the smell is quite sensationally heady.

Coriander *Coriandrum sativum:* Rather like caraway, coriander is a member of the parsley family, the plant growing to about two feet high with small pinkish flowers.

Coriander grows almost anywhere where the sun shines, grinding into a surprisingly dark spice, the seeds being very pale brown, not unlike peppercorns. Coriander adds a wonderful flavour to orange or lemon cakes having a slightly 'citrus' aroma and flavour. I understand that before toothpaste coriander seeds were chewed to freshen the breath – not much to do with cakes but interesting nonetheless.

Ginger *Zinigiber officinale:* The root or rhizome of the ginger plant can be used fresh, dried, preserved in syrup, crystallized or ground,

The ginger plant grows to about three feet high, with tall slender leaves and yellow flowers, and needs a tropical climate to grow well. The finest ginger comes from Jamaica.

There is an amazingly delicate almost citrus smell to a freshly sliced piece of root ginger, in contrast to the strongly aromatic smell of ground ginger. Traditionally ground ginger, crystallized or stem ginger has been used in Britain to make our very oldest of cakes, the gingerbread, so it is also good to know that ginger cakes can be eaten with the clearest of conscience as it is said to aid digestion!

Head of the Shop *Ras-el-Hanout:* No one can be certain what is in this wonderful Moroccan spice mixture as each shopkeeper has his own particular version, and so each batch varies from shop to shop.

Perhaps to clarify, it is possible to detail the sort of spices likely to have been included in a batch of Ras-el-Hanout, which are coriander, nutmeg, cloves, cardamom, cinnamon, ginger and nutmeg. In addition it is not unusual to find that lavender and rosebuds may also have been added.

Mace *Myristica fragrans;* **Nutmeg** *Myristica fragrans:* Mace and nutmeg grow together on the same tree; the blades of mace are wrapped around the outer shell of the nutmeg. Both spices are incredibly aromatic and wonderfully warming, although I always think mace is rather more 'citrus' and like to add it to lemon cakes.

The nutmeg tree grows to around 60 feet, with a large apricot like fruit surrounding the nut; the mace retains this lovely apricot colouring, while the nutmeg is dark brown.

Nutmeg is best ground freshly as needed, the flavour being far superior to any which has been stored ready ground. Both these spices have enjoyed steady popularity since the 17th century.

Mixed Spice: Not strictly speaking 'a spice' but a combination of spices most commonly used for cakes and puddings, and which has become a very traditional British mixture. Although it varies a little from retailer to retailer, the most common spices used are ground allspice, cinnamon, cloves, nutmeg and ginger.

Mixed spice is a quick and easy way of keeping some ready-to-use cake spices to hand, as it has to be admitted, it would be time consuming and very laborious grinding each of the individual spices every time you wanted to make a cake for tea. However, it is worth buying mixed spice in smallish quantities as it does not keep well and is infinitely better the fresher it is.

Poppy Seeds *Papavera somniferum:* Poppy seeds are widely used in the cooking of Eastern Europe, especially Poland and Russia.

Extracted from the seed heads when they are fully ripe, they can be easily shaken out and I was amazed to read that there are nearly one million poppy seeds in every 450g/1lb. Holland has become the centre for poppy seeds, growing the flowers with great success and producing the very best blue-black seeds. While the opium poppy does have the very best seeds for cooking, they are entirely free of any narcotic properties.

Saffron *Crocus sativus:* Saffron, an aromatic, deep orangey-red spice, was brought to Cornwall by the Phoenicians who exchanged it for tin, although it may actually have arrived here much earlier as the Arabs first introduced it into Europe in the 10th century.

Saffron Walden in Essex (Walden is Anglo-Saxon for field) was a flourishing centre for its growth as was Cambridgeshire where large fields of the purple saffron crocus (*crocus sativus*) were cultivated. Workers who spent their days tending the crocus became known as 'Crockers'. The highly labour intensive job, involved extracting the bright orange stamens by hand and spreading them out to dry. Most of what you buy today comes from Spain or Iran.

The most expensive and highly treasured spice in the world, it takes over 200,000 dried stigmas from around 70,000 crocus flowers to make a pound of saffron; it is therefore hardly surprising that it is so very precious.

Although costly it is still worthwhile buying the very best saffron you can find rather than some of the inferior varieties which are available. Remember how very little saffron you need to infuse in a small amount of water to achieve a delectable aroma and distinctive colour and it will seem slightly less extravagant.

Star Anise *Illicium verum:* Widely used in Chinese cookery, I find the star anise seed head, a pretty eight-pointed star, wonderfully decorative when baking.

The evergreen *Illicium verum* tree which is widely grown in China, not only has an important spice within its fruit, but its bark is used as incense.

The little brown seeds to be found in the points of the star anise, when ground down, also become an important part of the Chinese Five Spice Powder frequently used in their cooking.

Vanilla *Vanilla fragrans:* A native of Mexico, vanilla pods grow on vines. Production is very much a 'hands on' process, and the pods which are green initially, become the characteristic brown colour during curing which in turn brings out the aroma and flavour, with the whole procedure taking several months.

Originally the Aztecs blended vanilla with the beans from the pod of the cocoa plant, making chocolate rather as we know it today, but in 1520 when the Spanish conquered the Aztecs they named the pods 'vanilla' meaning 'little scabbard'. Although there have been many attempts to grow the pods outside of Mexico, none have been as successful, although I admit to preferring the Bourbon Vanilla from Madagascar, which has a truly sensational deep, dusky aroma.

One of the best ways to use the pods is to fill an airtight jar with caster sugar and tuck in 2 or 3 pods. They can be re-used many times; just keep topping up the jar as you use the sugar in sponges or cake recipes requiring vanilla flavouring.

BAKING AND MIXING METHODS

Creaming: Put the fat and sugar into a large bowl and using either a wooden spoon or hand mixer, beat until the two ingredients are thoroughly mixed together. The texture of the fat and sugar will become lighter, the colour paler. This is the way of adding air to most basic cake recipes.

Rubbing in: Generally this method is for rubbing fat into flour. Sift the flour and other ingredients as stated in the recipe, cut the fat into pieces adding it to the flour. Using only your fingertips and thumbs, to keep the ingredients cool, rub the ingredients together – you will see that the fat pieces become smaller and smaller until the mixture resembles fine breadcrumbs in texture.

Melting: This method is used in particular for gingerbreads, where the ingredients such as butter, sugar, treacle, syrup are melted gently over a low heat until they become completely amalgamated. It is however, important that the mixture is allowed to cool slightly before adding to the other ingredients so that it does not cook them.

In many recipes it is suggested that eggs are beaten into the melted mixture, again you can see how important it is to allow it to cool slightly before adding them or you will end up with scrambled eggs in the butter mixture.

Mixers: It is possible with some recipes to put all the ingredients into your mixer, switch on and hey presto – but the quality is never as good, sponges having quite large air holes and generally a poorer texture, but for some cakes this will simply be a matter of your preference and unimportant. In the case of shortcrust pastry, the base for several cakes, I find using the mixer method is excellent, particularly if like me you have warm hands, which are rather the death knoll for good pastry.

EQUIPMENT

It is actually possible to bake with very little equipment, the art of baking being basically a hands on procedure, but some items are essential.

Scales: A good set of scales are absolutely essential to enable careful weighing of the ingredients.

Wire cooling rack: It is important to own at least two of these and I find that generally the oblong ones are the most useful, as they can be used for both large cakes and lots of smaller buns. Quality is important; the prime thing to look out for is that they will be sufficiently strong to take the weight of large fruit cakes.

Sieve: A sieve is essential and a flour/icing shaker will be found to be very useful.

Spoons: Although you can use the spoons from your kitchen, it is possible to purchase very inexpensively a set of measuring spoons and I do think they are invaluable, I cannot imagine baking without a set. Try to buy sets incorporating 1/4 and 1/2 teaspoons sizes. In addition a metal tablespoon is necessary for some of the folding in procedures.

Knives: Knives, including large and small pallet knives, available from most cookery or kitchenware departments.

Wooden spoons: Inexpensive, easily available, you will need two or three in different sizes.

Lemon juicer: My favourite and certainly the simplest form of juicing a lemon, is a wooden squeezer, cut the lemon or orange in half and press and turn it in the middle of the flesh.

Grater: A multipurpose grater is indispensable and can be used for many tasks including grating nutmeg, so try to buy a four-sided grater, as these will give you the most options. Finally **greaseproof paper**, **cling film** and **foil** complete the essentials.

Apart from the above items it is unlikely that with a normal supply of things like bowls and saucepans which are found in all kitchens, you will need to purchase anything specifically for baking cakes.

CAKE TINS

Like most things in life, as with cake tins you really do get what you pay for. It is important to buy good quality, solid, beautifully made tins, although they need not necessarily be heavy, that will not only reward you with baking your cakes in superb style, but also last a lifetime if looked after properly.

Cake tins: A selection of tins will be useful and I suggest one 15cm/6in, 18cm/7 in and 20 cm/8in round tin, together with a 900g/2lb loaf tin, plus two sandwich tins, say 15cm/6in will be a good basic selection to which you can add.

Non-stick linings are good but personally I do not find them necessary, I like to line my tins with greaseproof paper anyway, giving the cake a little more protection. But if they are your preference, I would suggest lining them to ensure there is no possibility of sticking. For fruit cakes I find loose bottom tins preferable as removing the cake is made much simpler, lessening the risk of damaging your hard work.

Choosing the correct size of tin is probably one of the most important details in baking, too small a tin will cause problems as the cake will not have enough space to expand as it cooks, but too large a tin will result in a thin rather overcooked cake if care is not taken.

When deciding whether to use a round or square cake tin, it is important to note that the quantity of mixture prepared for a round tin, will need a square tin, an inch smaller in size i.e.: 18cm/7in round tin has the same capacity as a 15cm/6in square.

Baking trays: You will really need at least two good baking trays; recipes often require room for cakes to expand a little as they cook. Be sure to buy baking trays which are quite heavy and will not bend easily. They will conduct the heat better and lessen the chances of burning your cakes.

Do be sure that they will fit into the oven before you buy them. This may seem common sense but I am the person who once bought a table, which would not come through any door or window in the house. It remains in the garage to this day, a reminder that a 'bargain' turned into an embarrassment! We pot up plants on it.

Bun tin: You will find mention of bun tins in this book. These are the tins, which are normally sectioned into 12, suitable for making little fairy cakes, buns or cakes lined with pastry. They can be greased and used unlined, and indeed for pastry based cakes should be, but for buns and fairy cakes etc they can be lined with easily purchased greaseproof cake/bun tin liners. It is generally better to own at least two as most recipes make at least 18 cakes.

Swiss roll tin: A useful tin, oblong and shallow, not only suitable for making a swiss roll, but you will find the shape recommended in several recipes throughout the book.

Dariole moulds: Small individual tins, specifically for the baking of Madeleine Cakes. If you wish to bake this recipe, they are easily obtainable from any good kitchen equipment store.

Griddle (girdle): Rather less used nowadays, a griddle is a brilliant piece of equipment to own. I have always enjoyed making drop scones, ever since living half way up a moor in the Highlands of Scotland. Nothing seemed more enjoyable than baking while looking out at the falling snow, watching the bubbles rise before flipping over the really very delicious little cakes, to allow them to brown on the other side. Less commonly used the further south you go, I do think the griddle should enjoy a revival and lots of the recipes in this book, particularly the really old ones, require little imagination to think of cakes being baked on old ranges and over open fires.

That said a flat, heavy frying pan is a suitable alternative and you can always buy a griddle if you find yourself an enthusiast of griddle cakes.

LINING CAKE TINS

As you will see from the recipes in this book, I have detailed most of the cakes tins to be greased and lined and feel that I should briefly explain this procedure.

Firstly, it is very important when baking a cake which requires a long slow baking time in the oven, such as a rich fruit cake, not only to grease and line the tin with greaseproof paper, but also to tie a double layer of brown paper, with string, around the outside of the tin. This quite simply, stops the outer edge of the cake from cooking too quickly, which often results in a cake, which is dry on the edges, before it has finished cooking in the centre.

This is also why with the richer fruit cakes and cakes requiring some time in the oven, it may also be necessary not only to turn down the oven a little but to lay a piece of brown paper over the top of the cake tin, if the cake appears to be browning too rapidly.

900g/2lb loaf tin or bun tins: It is probably best to look in your local cookware shop or supermarket for ready made greaseproof liners, in the shape of these particular cakes, they are readily available and save a lot of difficult juggling around.

Round or square deep cake tin: Cut a double piece of greaseproof for the base by using the tin as a template, drawing around it and cutting it to fit snugly into the bottom of the tin. Then cut a strip of greaseproof paper long enough and deep enough to fit around the outer edges, allowing about 2.5cm/1in extra in depth. Lay the strip of greaseproof on the work surface and cut slits in one of the long edges to a depth of 2.5cm/1in approximately 1cm/1/2in apart. Grease lightly the cake tin and position the long strip around the inner edge of the tin, allowing the slits to sit on the bottom of the tin. Over these slits, position the double layer cut for the base of the tin. Now your tin will be fully lined and you will find that the slits you cut in the edging strip will have allowed the greaseproof paper to sit neatly around your tin.

It is generally best to peel lining paper carefully from a cake once it is cold, unless your recipe states otherwise, as it will help to prevent breaking the cake edges.

Sponge cake tins: These are generally shallow round tins or occasionally I like to use a ring tin but the preparation for both is the same.

Carefully lightly grease the surface of the tin and sprinkle it with a little flour. Then tip the tin from side to side to ensure that the surface is covered and that there are no gaps, otherwise your cake mixture will stick to the tin. Tip out any surplus flour, banging the tin gently. You can if you wish, lay a greaseproof circle in the base of the sandwich tin, I generally do, but it is not essential.

Baking trays: The preparation of these depends a little on what you are about to bake, a bun mixture can be baked on a lightly floured baking tray, but a sticky mixture such as ginger cakes and rock cakes, which are dropped or spooned onto the tray will benefit from lightly greasing the tins first.

INFORMATION ON BASIC INGREDIENTS

Yeast: A living plant, yeast in its low life form, produces carbon dioxide during fermentation and it is this gas which causes dough to rise by the formation of tiny bubbles, helped by the addition of a little sugar, which if creamed gently with the yeast and then set into a warm place, enables it to grow more quickly. You need to remember though that too much heat will kill the yeast, as it does during cooking, while too low a temperature slows the growth.

It is widely believed that the ancient Egyptians were responsible for discovering the raising powers of yeast, as before then all breads would have been unleavened. It was however, the French biologist, Louis Pasteur in the 19th century who really studied yeast and discovered the many other uses to which it could be applied including Vitamin B and medicinally in the manufacture of drugs including antibiotics.

While the use of yeast is strongly associated in our minds with bread making, it should be remembered that a great many of our traditional cakes are yeast based and there are a lot of recipes in the yeast section of the book which I hope you will find interesting. Yeast based cakes have appeared in so many cookery books and story books over the years that their place in history in undeniable, the famous Simnel Cake was once yeast based and of course, many Harvest Cakes were dough based, so historically yeast cakes were the forerunners of so many of our modern cakes.

Brewers' yeast: Also known as Ale Barm or Beer Barm, the yeast is the froth, which forms on top of the liquid as it ferments. This is the oldest type of 'Bakers' Yeast, it can however, be very bitter, being the product which is discarded during the making of beer or ale. The fermented liquid is the part we enjoy drinking.

Compressed yeast: These are yeast plant cells, compressed into a block, bound together with the addition of a little starch. Perhaps the best form of yeast to use in the baking of cakes, giving an excellent flavour and being simple to use.

Dried yeast: This form of yeast is relatively modern, convenient to use and sold in packets which have a long shelf life.

Baking powder: The combination of alkaline and acid substances found in baking powder, when moistened, produce carbon dioxide, which in turn will make a cake rise. These substances are bicarbonate of soda and cream of tartar or tartaric acid, which when combined with a stabilizing ingredient such as arrowroot, cornflour or ground rice, enables it to be safely stored ready for use. It is not difficult to imagine how, when this product first became available in 1846, it must have seemed truly remarkable, totally transforming the cook's cake making sessions, as before that time the only way to make a cake rise without the use of yeast, involved arm aching whisking of eggs and sugar, sometimes for an hour or more.

Bicarbonate of soda: a raising agent, which is often used in cakes, which include honey or treacle, such as gingerbreads. It also works well with buttermilk or sour milk.

Buttermilk: Helps to lift heavier recipes. It can be easily bought in delicatessens or some of the larger supermarkets.

Sour milk: This can be made at home by adding a teaspoon of lemon juice and allowing the milk to curdle. Alternatively, the milk can be simply left in a warm atmosphere until it becomes sour, when it should be placed in a refrigerator until needed. Sour milk, like buttermilk, helps to lift heavier recipes.

Eggs: Personally I always try to use free range eggs, simply because I feel a lot less guilty if I know that the welfare of the hen has been taken into consideration, allowing them to run around in conditions which ensure a happy chicken. When using eggs this will be your personal choice.

The important thing to bear in mind however, is that you should use large (size 1 or 2) for most recipes unless otherwise stated and always lightly beat them before using. Whether you simply keep your eggs in a cool place or the refrigerator, they should always be at room temperature before using in a recipe, as very cold eggs are likely to cause the mixture to curdle.

Sugar: It was during Elizabethan times that sugar became more widely available at least for the more affluent families; honey being the most common sweetener up until then, sugar having been available only in limited quantities and at a very high price.

Sold mainly in cones, pieces would be broken and pounded, a little tool called a Nipper was used to cut off portions of the cone. It was not however, until much later at the end of the 17th century that sugar came into its own being used to sweeten tea and other food items.

Coming mainly from sugar cane and sugar beet, the largest source is the cane variety, grown mainly in tropical climates. Sugar beet, which is often fed to animals in Britain, is grown in temperate climates but the resulting extracted sugars from either cane or beet are absolutely identical.

Caster sugar: Fine white sugar, excellent for sponges, particularly suited to creaming methods.

Granulated sugar: A coarser sugar, which can be used for cakes and will cream quite well, but the texture will result in speckled cake tops if used in sponges. It is most commonly used for sweetening drinks and sprinkling over food.

Demerara sugar: A very coarse pale brown sugar, with good flavour. Rubs in well and is particularly suited for use in the making of gingerbreads.

Soft brown sugars: Either dark brown or pale brown, they give a good flavour and cream well, not unlike fudge or caramel to taste.

Muscovado sugar: Dark brown or pale brown, it is strongly flavoured and excellent for fruit cakes.

Jaggery: A dark brown sugar made from the sap of the date palm trees.

Plain flour: The most common variety used in fruit cakes, it has a low gluten content, which produces softer textured cakes. Plain flour having no added raising agent, is particularly suited to the cakes which are not required to rise very much, such as a fruit cake. A raising agent can be added, according to the quantity in any particular recipe and this method does at least give you complete control. Generally the raising agent used will be baking powder.

Strong plain flour is more suitable for use in the fruit tea breads and buns as it has very high gluten content, but is unsuitable for cakes in general.

Self-raising flour: This is simply plain flour to which a raising agent has already been added, baking powder therefore generally being unnecessary. However care should be taken when using this flour, as you have no control over the amount of rise it will give to a cake.

Wholemeal or wheatmeal flour: Particularly suitable for whole food cakes having a lot of the husk of the grains retained, they are therefore considered healthier. They can be bought in both plain and self-raising flour varieties.

There are many other types of flour; rye, buckwheat, cornflour, rice flour and ingredients used in place of flour, mochiko rice flour, cornmeal, polenta and farina.

Do note: It is particularly important to sift flour when adding baking powder, bicarbonate of soda, spices or other such ingredients, as this is the only way of ensuring they are evenly distributed. Finally, flour must be kept sealed or in an airtight container and stored in dry conditions.

Fats: Butter or soft margarine are the most widely used fats for cakes, but in this book you will come across many recipes using lard or pork dripping and even in one or two cases 'flead' which is the small droplets of fat, lining the stomach of a pig, albeit they are very old recipes! However, where such fats are used, they are intrinsic to the particular recipe.

Personally I prefer butter for cakes because I think it gives an excellent flavour and certainly for fruit cakes, it adds to the texture and keeping qualities. However, many of the soft margarines on the market now, do make really good cakes and are less expensive for everyday cooking. Butter should always be used at room temperature for baking, unless otherwise specified.

Ghee: Clarified butter used in Indian cookery.

Black treacle: Very dark, very strong and can dominate cakes, ideal for some gingerbreads or rich dark fruit cakes. The flavour mellows over a period of time.

Golden syrup: Lighter and stickier. Very sweet, ideal for use in gingerbreads, I often use it half and half with black treacle, giving a more delicate and less dominating flavour.

Nuts: When purchasing and storing nuts, it is important not only to buy the best quality you can find, but also to adhere strictly to the best before date and storage instructions as nuts have relatively short shelf lives.

Vine fruits: The varieties are endless but again, try to seek out the best – it will always be worthwhile.

PORTION SIZES

This chart gives you an idea of the number of slices which can be cut from a particular size of cake, all the tins detailed below are round.

Cakes baked in square tins are generally cut into smaller portions, the shape and size of which, where relevant, will be indicated in a particular recipe.

13cm / 5in cake tin approx. 4-6 slices	20cm / 8in cake tin approx. 10-12 slices
15cm / 6in cake tin approx. 6-7 slices	23cm / 9in cake tin approx. 12-14 slices
18cm / 7in cake tin approx. 8-9 slices	25.5cm / 10in cake tin approx. 14-16 slices

CONVERSION TABLES / MEASUREMENT

1/8 inch / 3mm	1 3/4 inch / 4.5cm	5 1/2 inches / 13.5cm	9 1/2 inches / 24cm
1/4 inch / 5mm	2 inches / 5cm	6 inches / 15cm	10 inches / 25.5cm
1/2 inch / 1cm	2 1/2 inches / 6cm	6 1/2 inches / 16cm	11 inches / 28cm
3/4 inch / 2cm	3 inches / 7.5cm	7 inches / 18cm	12 inches / 30cm
1 inch / 2.5cm	3 1/2 inches / 9cm	7 1/2 inches / 19cm	
1 1/4 inch / 3cm	4 inches / 10cm	8 inches / 20cm	
1 1/2 inch / 4cm	5 inches / 13cm	9 inches / 23cm	

VOLUME

2fl oz / 50ml	20fl oz/ 1 pint / 570ml
3fl oz / 75ml	1 1/4 pints / 725ml
4fl oz / 100-125ml	1 3/4 pints / 1 litre
5fl oz / 1/4 pint / 150ml	2 pints / 1.2 litres
10fl oz/ 1/2 pint / 275ml	2 1/2 pints / 1.5 litres
15fl oz/ 3/4 pint / 425ml	4 pints / 2.25 litres

OVEN TEMPERATURES

120°C / 250°F / Gas Mark 1/2	190°C / 375°F / Gas Mark 5
140°C / 275°F / Gas Mark 1	200°C / 400°F / Gas Mark 6
150°C / 300°F / Gas Mark 2	220°C / 425°F / Gas Mark 7
160°C / 325°F / Gas Mark 3	230°C / 450°F / Gas Mark 8
180°C / 350°F / Gas Mark 4	240°C / 475°F / Gas Mark 9

Note: When using a fan oven, they can be a bit of a law unto themselves and I find with mine that setting the Centigrade about 10 degrees lower than suggested in the recipe, gives the right result.

WEIGHTS

1/2oz / 10g	2 1/2oz / 60g	6oz / 175g	12oz / 350g
3/4oz / 20g	3oz / 75g	7oz / 200g	1lb / 450g
1oz / 25g	4oz / 115g	8oz / 225g	1 1/2 lb / 700g
1 1/2oz / 40g	4 1/2oz / 125g	9oz / 250g	2lbs / 900g
2oz / 50g	5oz / 150g	10oz / 275g	3lbs / 1.35kg

Please note: the translation of grams to ounces may vary very slightly between recipes and bakers i.e. 110-115g is the equivalent of 4oz which is quite acceptable as grams are a very small measurement, and this will not affect the cakes.

BASIC RECIPES

PUFF PASTRY

Makes 450g/1lb

450g/1lb plain flour
1/2 teaspoon salt

450g/1lb butter
4fl oz/100ml very cold water

Sift the flour and salt into a large bowl and add 50g/2oz of the slightly softened butter, rub into the flour until it resembles fine breadcrumb texture.

Add enough water to form a soft dough and turn the pastry out onto a lightly floured board, kneading gently until smooth.

Roll the pastry into an oblong and dot half the remaining butter onto one half. Fold the other half of the pastry over the buttered area and roll out the pastry again into an oblong, repeating the process with the remaining butter. Wrap the pastry in cling film and leave in a cool place such as the refrigerator for about 30 minutes to allow it to settle.

Next stage: Roll the dough into an oblong again, being careful not to let any of the butter break through the surface of the pastry and then fold it into three and return in cling film to the refrigerator for a further 45 minutes, it is this folding which gives the pastry its characteristic layers.

Repeat the process twice more and then the pastry is ready to use. You will be able to see the layers you have formed in the pastry dough, during all the folding and rolling.

Bake in accordance with the recipe for which you have prepared the pastry dough.

Note: I feel compelled to say at this stage that there is absolutely no crime however, in buying one of the excellent frozen or chilled packs of puff pastry which are readily available in supermarkets today, as it is simply impossible to make a good puff pastry without taking considerable time and trouble.

SHORTCRUST PASTRY   *Makes 450g/1lb*

450g/1lb plain flour
1/2 teaspoon salt
175g/6oz butter

50g/2oz white vegetable fat or lard
3 to 4 tablespoons very cold water

Sift the flour and salt into a bowl and add the butter and vegetable fat or lard, which should have been chilled and cut into small pieces. Rub it lightly into the flour with your fingertips until it resembles fine breadcrumbs and then add a little of the water, stirring with a pallet knife. Add a little more water until the mixture forms into soft (but not sticky) dough.

Wrap the pastry in cling film and store in the refrigerator until required.

Note: It is important when making short crust pastry to keep your hands as cool as possible. The surface on which the pastry is prepared and rolled should also be cold; marble or stainless steel is particularly suitable. In addition the pastry dough should be handled as little as possible, otherwise you will end up with very heavy pastry.

YEAST BREAD DOUGH BASE   *Makes approximately 450g/1lb dough base*

20g/3/4oz fresh yeast
2 teaspoons caster sugar
175ml/6fl oz lukewarm milk

450g/1lb plain flour
    (White or wholemeal depending on recipe)
3/4 teaspoon salt

In a small bowl cream the yeast and sugar together and add the lukewarm milk, stirring thoroughly. Set aside in a warm place to allow the yeast to work and froth to develop for about 10 minutes.

Sift the flour and salt into a large warm bowl, making a well in the centre.

Pour the yeast mixture into the flour, stir with a pallet knife and then using your hands, mix the dough together until a ball is formed.

On a lightly floured surface, knead thoroughly for 5 minutes until smooth and elastic. Then use as required in the recipe for which you have made the dough base.

Note: It is important when preparing dough not to allow any of the ingredients to become cold, yeast dies if it becomes either too hot (as in cooking) or if it becomes very cold it slows down the active ingredient.

DANISH PASTRY DOUGH

Not an easy dough to make, well worth the effort, but best approached in three stages.

5 teaspoons dried yeast	60g/2oz melted butter
1 teaspoon sugar	2 large eggs
125ml/4fl oz lukewarm water	250ml/8 fl oz milk
	A little extra flour if needed
450g/1lb plain flour	
90g/3oz caster sugar	250g/8oz slightly softened butter
pinch of salt	

Put the yeast, sugar and water into a small jug, stir and set aside.

In a large bowl, sift the flour and making a well in the centre, add the sugar, salt, melted butter, eggs and milk and finally the frothy yeast mixture.

Using a pallet knife, stir the ingredients until you have gathered all the mixture together, lift the dough onto a lightly floured surface and gently knead until smooth, wrap it in cling film and refrigerate for about 30 minutes.

Meanwhile, place the butter between two sheets of greaseproof paper and roll out to about 20x18cm/8x7in. Unwrap the now chilled dough onto a lightly floured surface and roll out to about 23x40cm/9x16in. With a narrow edge towards you, place the butter onto the lower half of the dough and bring the top half down over the butter. Press the edges together and roll the dough back out into a rectangle. Roll out the dough into a large oblong and fold the bottom 1/3 up onto the middle 1/3, bringing the top 1/3 down over the other two sections. Roll out into an oblong again and repeat the above folding three more times, putting the layers into the dough.

Wrap the dough in cling film and place in the fridge for about 30 minutes to chill and rest.

SMALL CAKES AND DOUGHNUTS

One thing immediately apparent in this cake section, is the diversity of ingredients, providing a range of flavours, aromas and visual delights. When you see the cakes come out of the oven you can take in the smells and tastes of another world; it just can't be surpassed as a baking experience.

In addition, many of the cakes have delightful stories attached to them; the little French Madeleines or the two contradictory versions of the Spanish *Mantecados de Soria* cakes. Maybe a story which makes you smile, after all cakes should give pleasure, so perhaps the story of the cake-eating ghost, who I am quite sure would love the little Indian cakes, *Gulab Jamun*, they may even make the ghost smile. Frequently cakes are for some particular annual celebration, such as the Swedish Semla Cake, baked for Lent or the Finnish *Runebergintorttu* which celebrates the birth of Finland's national poet Runeberg.

The subject of doughnuts became really intriguing as I began to realise just how many different ones are baked throughout the world, each with its own, albeit similar recipe and its own particular shape and identity. How often they pop up in the world, even in some unlikely corners and Hawaii is no exception.

Not unlike batter cakes, the ingredients are usually just flour, sugar, butter, sometimes with the addition of eggs and milk, but without exception the cakes are always fried and usually sprinkled in sugar, making it almost impossible not to lick your fingers after eating a doughnut.

When reading through the following recipes, I do hope you will find their individual stories intriguing and be tempted to bake some of these deliciously sticky little cakes.

MACAROONS

The large number of pâtisserie shops found in each town or village in France, makes it impossible, whilst holidaying in this wonderfully foodie country, to avoid cakes.

But imagine my amazement when rounding the corner of a cobbled street in the lovely town of Quimper in Brittany, I came upon the beautifully decorated tea shop of *La Macaronerie*, Rolland Padou, whose window displays were simply stunning. The centrepiece was a pyramid of macaroons several feet high, in all colours and flavours, a bright green pistachio, the zingy pink of *framboise*, a pale mauve of *miel de lavendre*, a yellow *citron* and orange *fleur d'oranger*. So the macaroons we finally came to bake for photographer, Michelle for my book suddenly came to life, making it well worth the time and care spent on preparation.

150g/5oz icing sugar	**Butter Cream filling**
115g/4oz finely ground almonds	115g/4oz unsalted butter
3 large egg whites at room temperature	115g/4oz icing sugar
25g/1oz caster sugar	
Colourings and flavourings of your choice	

Lay greaseproof paper onto two or three large baking trays and draw circles of approximately 2.5cm/1in in diameter onto the sheets, allowing at least 4cm/1 1/2in between each one.

Sieve the icing sugar into a bowl and stir in the ground almonds.

In a clean bowl whisk the egg whites until stiff, add the caster sugar and whisk until completely incorporated and the whites are standing in peaks. Gently fold in the icing sugar and ground almond mixture.

At this stage we found it easiest to divide the macaroon mixture into two or three smaller bowls to which we added our chosen colourings and flavourings, being careful to stir gently but thoroughly so as not to lose the texture of the mixture. We used 1 heaped teaspoon of cocoa for one third of the mixture, one third coloured pink and one third yellow.

Using a large piping bag with a 2.5cm/1in plain nozzle, pipe the macaroon batters onto the circles on the baking trays. Set them aside for about 1 hour, to settle and form a slight skin on the surface of the cakes.

Heat the oven to 160°C/325°F/Gas Mark 3 and when up to temperature, bake each of the trays for about 10 or 15 minutes, leaving the oven door slightly ajar.

Remove the cakes from the oven and transfer the greaseproof sheets onto cooling racks.

When the macaroons are cold, carefully lift them from the greaseproof using a spatula and gently place onto the wire racks until you are ready to pair them together.

Finally, prepare the butter cream by whisking the softened butter with the icing sugar until pale and smooth and use to pair the macaroon halves together. Place the cakes into a refrigerator until required, allowing back to room temperature before serving and enjoying.

TEISEN BERFFRO /ABERFFRAW CAKES

WALES   *Makes 12*

These cakes are still baked today in the small village of Aberffraw, which overlooks the sea on the Isle of Anglesey, and which was once the home of Welsh princes. Traditionally baked in scallop shells, they are rich and buttery but are no less delicious if you use a cutter instead of shells.

175g/6oz butter
175g/6oz caster sugar
175g/8 oz self-raising flour

Topping
Caster sugar

Preheat the oven to 160°C/325°F/Gas Mark 3.

Cream together the butter and sugar until pale and creamy.

Sift the flour before slowly adding to the butter mix, stirring to form a soft dough.

On a lightly floured board, roll the dough out to about 1 cm/1/2in thick before cutting into 4cm/2in rounds with a plain cutter, this should make about 12 cakes.

Place the cakes on a lightly greased baking tray and cook in the centre of the oven for 10-15 minutes or until golden brown.

When baked, lift them carefully onto a wire rack to cool and then sprinkle with caster sugar before serving.

ALMOND HORNS

SWITZERLAND   *Makes 10*

The delectable combinations of fillings, toppings and indeed the basic cake mixtures used in Swiss cakes makes them really very special. While the ingredients are often relatively simple, the way in which they are used is artistic both in shape and design such as these Almond Horns or Crescents. They are easily made, and all that is required is a little patience.

450g/1lb caster sugar
225g/8oz ground almonds
4 large egg whites
100g/4oz flaked almonds lightly chopped

Topping
100g/4oz chocolate

Preheat the oven to 425°F/220°C/Gas Mark 7 and line two baking trays with non-stick baking paper.

Measure the sugar, ground almonds and egg whites into a bowl and using a pallet knife, stir until they form a ball. Using your hands, gather it together and lift onto a work surface, which has been lightly dusted with icing sugar.

Roll small pieces of the mixture into snakes about 6cm/2¹/2in long and roll them in the flaked almonds before laying them onto the baking trays and forming them into crescent shapes.

Cook in the oven for about 10 minutes until pale golden brown.

Allow to become completely cold. Melt the chocolate in a small bowl over a saucepan of simmering water and dip each end of the crescents into the melted chocolate before putting them onto a wire rack to set.

KRINGLAS / FIGURE OF EIGHT CAKES

NORWAY   *Makes 24*

There are many different recipes for the Kringla Cakes, but the shape never alters. Similarly, the number of cakes you can make from any recipe will vary, simply because there is no golden rule to the size of the cakes, the smaller the cakes, the more you will get from your dough.

125g/4¹/2oz softened butter	1 teaspoon vanilla extract
175g/6oz caster sugar	450g/1lb plain flour
1 egg	¹/2 teaspoon baking soda
250ml/9fl oz single cream	3 level teaspoons baking powder

Preheat the oven to 200°C/400°F/Gas Mark 6.

Using a hand held mixer, on a high speed, cream the butter and sugar until pale and fluffy. On the slowest speed, add the rest of the ingredients a little at a time, until a soft smooth ball of dough is formed. Wrap the cake mix in cling film and store in the refrigerator for at least 4 hours, preferably longer. The dough must be refrigerated, to make it easier to handle.

Take the dough from the refrigerator and on a lightly floured surface, break off some small pieces about the size of a walnut (or a little larger if preferred) and roll into long strips. Shape them into figure of eights and place onto the baking trays. Leave to rise in a cool place for about an hour before putting them into the preheated oven and baking for 10-15 minutes or until golden brown. Best eaten fresh from the oven.

MADELEINES

FRANCE   *Makes about 20 cakes*

While both are made from the lightest of sponges, English Madeleines, which are baked in little dariole moulds, before brushing with jam and rolling in coconut, are very different to French ones. These little shell shaped cakes have become one of the delights of the traditional French tea table and on a recent holiday in France, Madeleines were prominently displayed both in smaller village bakeries and larger ones in the cities. They are supposedly named for Madeleine Palmier, a French pastry chef, who during the 19th century worked in Commercy, a town in the Lorraine region of France.

150g/5oz butter	150g/5oz self-raising flour
3 large eggs	25g/1oz ground almonds
150g/5oz caster sugar	Finely grated rind of an orange

Preheat the oven to 220°C/425°F/Gas 7.

Grease the Madeleine tins before lightly dusting with flour.

Melt the butter in a small pan and set aside to cool slightly. In a large bowl whisk the eggs and sugar until thick and pale. Finally, using a large metal spoon, fold in the flour, ground almonds and orange rind alternately with the melted butter. It is essential to be as gentle as possible, to keep in all the air you have just whisked in.

Spoon some mixture into each of the Madeleine moulds, place on a baking tray for ease of handling and bake in the centre of the oven for about 10 minutes or until well risen and golden brown. Do not worry if they peak slightly in the centre.

Immediately they are removed from the oven, gently tip them out of their moulds onto a wire rack and allow to cool. They are best eaten on the day of baking.

SEMLA CAKES

Makes 10-12

There are several wonderful tales connected with this cake but perhaps the most dramatic was that, as a result of King Adolf Frederick's death in 1771, following an enormous meal, finished off by eating a Semla bun, they were banned. The citizens became convinced the bun had been the cause of his death and it was not until half a century later that they began to appear in Swedish Lenten feasting, traditionally served with warmed milk and occasionally put into a bowl and steeped in warm milk.

Baked in several small pieces or a large round bun, a Semla is hollowed out and filled with almond paste, whipped cream and sprinkled over with cinnamon before serving. Known as 'Fat Tuesday Buns', Semlas were originally baked for eating on Fettisdagen or Shrove Tuesday, before the Lenten fasting begins but they are now a common sight on bakers' counters, appearing as soon as the Christmas festivities are over.

50g/2oz butter	**Filling**
250ml/1/2 pint lukewarm milk	200g/8oz almond paste
25g/1oz fresh yeast	Whipping cream as liked
100g/4oz caster sugar	Icing sugar
Pinch of salt	
2 eggs, lightly beaten	
200g/6oz plain flour	

Preheat the oven to 200°C/400°F/Gas Mark 6 and lightly grease a baking tray.

In a small saucepan slowly melt the butter in the lukewarm milk. Place the yeast in a medium sized bowl and pour a little of the milk and butter on to it, stirring to dissolve the yeast before adding the sugar, a pinch of salt and lastly the remaining buttery milk. Beat with a wooden spoon, adding half the egg and all the flour a little at a time, before turning onto a floured surface and kneading until the dough is smooth and elastic. The dough is now ready to place into a clean bowl and covered with a cloth before leaving in a warm place to double in size – about 1 hour.

After the dough has risen, turn it out onto a floured work surface and knead briefly before breaking into 10 or 12 evenly sized pieces. Place the little buns onto the baking tray and leave in a warm place once more to double in size – about 30 minutes.

Brush the tops with the remaining beaten egg before cooking in the centre of the oven. The cakes will cook quite quickly and it is essential to check after 10 minutes but if not ready, keep checking every 5 minutes until golden brown. Remove from the oven and place on a metal cooling rack before covering them with a clean cloth and leaving to become completely cold. Finally cut a slice from the top of each cake and spoon out the centres mixing them with the almond paste; place an equal portion back into each cake, swirling a little whipped cream on top before replacing the lid and lightly dusting with icing sugar.

GULAB JAMUN

INDIA   *Makes about 20 cakes*

The history of the Indian subcontinent is amazingly complex; the Portuguese, Persians and of course, the British are amongst many nationalities who brought new ideas and customs with them when they settled there which in turn influenced the food, the ingredients and finished dishes.

While researching Indian cakes I stumbled upon the story of a cake-eating ghost; a British soldier who died from ill health in the Northern Indian state of Bihar in 1906, was buried in the town of Gaya. However, to this day the restless ghost is said to ask passers-by for a cup of tea and a piece of cake. Local residents have many stories and superstitions about the ghost, but perhaps the most fascinating tale of all, is that he is quickly 'calmed' if tea and cake are placed on his grave, which miraculously always disappears, doubtless eaten by the consoled ghost.

Perhaps one of the very best cakes to offer the 'ghost' would be these wonderfully aromatic little cakes, steeped in a cardamom-flavoured syrup and finished with a sprinkling of rose water. Everything about them typifies 'an Indian delicacy'.

Syrup	**Dough**
275g/10oz granulated sugar	60g/2^{1}/2 oz self-raising flour
450ml/3/4 pint water	20g/3/4 oz semolina
8 cardamom pods	2 teaspoons baking powder
	200g/7oz dried milk powder
	150ml/1/4 pint milk
	Rose water

Measure the sugar and water into a small saucepan and bring to the boil. Add the cardamom pods, lightly crushed (use a rolling pin). Allow the syrup to simmer for about 10 minutes, by which time it will be wonderfully fragrant. Remove from the heat and allow to cool.

Measure the self-raising flour, semolina, baking powder and dried milk powder into a large bowl and add the milk, while stirring with a large spoon, adding a little more milk if necessary until a firm dough mixture is formed.

On a lightly floured surface, knead the dough until smooth. Divide into about 20 equally sized pieces and roll them into little balls.

Fill a medium sized saucepan a third full with cooking oil and heat until it begins to smoke a little. Break off a tiny piece of the cake mixture and drop it into the oil, when it is hot enough the dough will rise to the surface surrounded by tiny bubbles. Using a metal slotted spoon, lower 2 or 3 of the little cakes into the oil and allow them to brown before turning them over; they will cook quite quickly. Lift them from the oil onto a plate covered in kitchen paper to drain.

As soon as they are all cooked but while still hot, transfer them to a serving plate and pour over the cardamom syrup. Finish with a little rose water poured over each cake.

MANTECADOS DE SORIA /
BUTTER CAKES OF SORIA

SPAIN   *Makes 12*

It is hard for me to think about Spanish cakes without recalling a case of 'dreadful misunderstanding'. Inego, a charming young man from southern Spain, was staying with us for the summer and one evening while sitting down to dinner, we talked about food and the gateau I had made. The main course however, was beef in beer and I was very surprised when Inego toyed with his food, saying he wasn't hungry.

Later I produced the gateau and asked him if he would like a slice, which brought a large grin to his face. He explained that gateau (gato) in Spanish means cat and poor Inego thought his meal had been an English delicacy – cat in beer.

But here we have a Spanish delicacy – Mantecados. Spanish cakes are often baked with ground almonds rather than flour and have the addition of their wonderfully aromatic citrus fruits. Olive oil is often used instead of butter in such things as sponge cakes and to my astonishment it really does work, but why am I surprised when butter becomes liquid when subjected to heat – just a different liquid?

Having found that these little cakes are always made with butter and piled into little pastry cases before baking, I then stumble upon another excellent recipe saying that you should never use butter only lard. However my chosen version uses butter.

100g/4oz butter	2 large eggs
100g/4oz caster sugar	50g/2oz self-raising flour

Preheat the oven to 180°C/350°F/Gas Mark 4.

Cream the butter and caster sugar with an electric hand whisk until very pale and creamy.

Lightly beat the eggs before stirring a little at a time into the mixture, finally stirring in the flour.

Using a bun tin for 12 cakes, line them with paper cases and spoon an equal amount of mixture into each case.

Place in the centre of the oven and cook for about 10 to 15 minutes until the top when pressed gently, feels springy. Allow the cakes to cool on a wire rack.

BASBOUSA / SEMOLINA CAKE

EGYPT

In Egypt they have a superb range of absolutely delectable small and usually very sweet cakes. Basbousa, cut into diamonds and topped with a blanched almond, is finished with lemon sugar syrup, giving it its characteristic 'stickiness'. Semolina cakes are popular within many countries in the Middle East, Egypt of course, but also Turkey, Greece and Cyprus all have their variations. Cut into squares or diamonds before serving, not only is the cake steeped in very rich syrup but each portion is decorated with a whole blanched almond.

What does not vary though is the inclusion of yogurt, either in the cake mixture or in some cases the cake will be served with yogurt to accompany it.

115g/4oz butter	**Syrup**
175g/6oz caster sugar	200g/7oz caster sugar
150g/5oz semolina (farina)	150ml/1/4 pint water
150g/5oz desiccated coconut	2 tablespoons fresh lemon juice
1 teaspoon baking powder	
2 eggs, lightly beaten	**Decoration**
1 teaspoon vanilla extract	Blanched almonds
175ml/6fl oz plain yogurt	

Preheat oven to 180°C/350°F/Gas Mark 4 and grease and line a 20x30cm/8x12in shallow cake tin.

Using a hand held electric mixer, cream together the butter and sugar until light and fluffy. Add the semolina, coconut, baking powder, eggs, vanilla extract and yogurt, stirring thoroughly until mixed.

Spoon the mixture into the cake tin, gently smoothing the top with the back of the spoon. Bake in the oven for about 25-30 minutes, or until the cake is springy to touch.

While the cake is cooking put the sugar, water and lemon into a small saucepan and bring to the boil. Simmer for about 10 minutes until it becomes syrupy, set aside to cool.

When the cake is cooked, leaving it in the tin, evenly pour over the syrup and set aside to become completely cold.

Finally, cut the cake into diamonds and top each portion with an almond.

BRITISH COLUMBIAN NUT BROWNIES

CANADA

Makes 9

The recipe for Canadian nut brownies appeared where I least expected it; in fact while reading an English cake book, dated 1932.

150g/5oz dates	1 teaspoon vanilla extract
115g/4oz walnut halves	50g/2oz cocoa
50g/2oz raisins	115g/4oz plain flour
2 eggs	1/2 teaspoon baking powder
175g/6oz caster sugar	

Preheat oven to 180°C/350°F/Gas Mark 4.

Stone the dates and cut into small pieces. Chop the walnuts finely. Set them aside.

Whisk the eggs, add the sugar and vanilla extract and whisk again until light and fluffy.

Gently stir in the flour and baking powder, ensuring it does not become lumpy. Finally, stir in the fruit and nut pieces.

Spoon the mixture into a greased, shallow baking tin approximately 23x18 cm/9x7in and cook for about 15-20 minutes, checking that it remains slightly springy to touch. Be careful not to overcook the cake or it will be dry.

Finally, cut the cake into fingers while still hot and coat with sieved icing sugar. Traditionally, the little cakes are rolled in icing sugar which you may wish to try, but I found that they broke up very easily, and appeared to be equally delicious simply sprinkled.

Best left for 24 hours before eating for the flavour to develop properly.

TULUMBA TATLISI / FLUTED FRITTERS

TURKEY

Makes 6

Being a great pastry chef has its disadvantages, as my dear friend Sally Baxter found out when she went on holiday to Turkey recently. Did she really imagine that I wouldn't ask her about Turkish cakes? Fortunately, she was more than happy to investigate and even taste (what a wonderful excuse) as many cakes as possible for me.

Syrup	**Dough**
450ml/3/4 pint water	25g/1oz butter
350g/12oz sugar	300ml/1/2 pint water
Juice and zest of a lemon	225g/8oz flour
	Pinch of salt
	4 eggs, lightly beaten
	Oil to fry the fritters

Measure the water, sugar and lemon juice and zest into a small saucepan, bring to the boil and simmer for 15 minutes. Put aside to cool.

In a medium saucepan, melt the butter in the water and bring to the boil. Add the flour and salt before turning to a low heat. Stirring constantly with a wooden spoon, cook for 5 to 6 minutes. Set aside to cool before adding the eggs a little at a time, beating hard to incorporate them into the dough.

Turn the mixture onto a floured worktop and knead for about 10 minutes.

Heat some oil in a frying pan. Put the dough into a large piping bag and pipe 4–5cm lengths of dough into the hot oil, a few at a time. Fry until golden brown, lifting out with a slotted spoon, draining well before dropping them into the cool syrup. Leave for about 10-15 minutes before lifting them out and piling onto a serving dish. Best eaten the same day as cooking.

POLVORONES

MEXICO   *Makes 10*

From the Spanish word *polvo* meaning dust, Polvorones are so named because they are extremely delicate and crumble easily. That is why they are often sold individually wrapped in coloured tissue paper, the ends of which are shredded. Brought to Mexico by the Spanish, these delicate little cakes have firmly established themselves as an essential part of any celebration table. However, there is an exception, weddings, when these delectable little cakes are wrapped in white and silver paper.

The fat used in the recipe is by tradition lard, but with the increased availability of vegetable shortening, I found the flavour much improved with the use of half vegetable shortening and half fresh butter.

225g/8oz caster sugar	350g/12oz self-raising flour
115g/4oz vegetable shortening	1/2 teaspoon ground cinnamon
115g/4oz butter	225g/8oz icing sugar
2 eggs, lightly beaten	1 teaspoon ground cinnamon

Preheat the oven to 160°C/325°F/Gas Mark 3.

Using a hand mixer, cream the sugar, vegetable shortening and butter together until light and fluffy.

Mix slowly while adding the eggs, flour and cinnamon a little at a time until the mixture forms a firm ball of dough.

Using your fingers break off evenly sized pieces, rolling them into balls and placing them onto a lined baking tray. Gently flatten them a little. They should measure about 11/2-2 inches in diameter.

Bake for about 10-15 minutes until pale golden brown. Using a spatula lift them onto a cooling rack and dust quite heavily with the icing sugar and ground cinnamon.

Leave to become completely cold before wrapping in tissue to display on your festive table.

RUNEBERGINTORTTU / RUNEBERG CAKES

FINLAND   *Makes 12*

Every year on the 5th February the birth of Finland's national poet, J. L. Runeberg is commemorated by cake eating, including these delightful eponymous little cakes. Recipes do vary slightly, some including dried breadcrumbs, but the one I found most successful used flour and ground almonds giving a very moist result.

The individual Runeberg cake tins are very difficult to buy outside of Scandinavia but I found the English Madeleine cake tins to be perfect, even if the sides do slope a little.

125g/4oz softened butter	**Topping**
125g/4oz soft pale brown sugar	250g/8oz icing sugar
2 eggs, lightly beaten	1 egg white
125g/4oz self-raising flour	
60g/2oz ground almonds	Jar of red jam of your choice

Preheat the oven to 180°C/350°F/Gas Mark 4.

Grease and lightly flour the cake tins and place onto a baking tray ready to fill with mixture.

Using a hand held electric mixer at high speed, cream the butter and sugar until light and fluffy. On the lowest speed add the remaining ingredients a little at a time, to ensure the mixture does not curdle.

Fill the cake tins to about three quarters full and place them back onto the baking tray before putting them into the oven. After about 20 minutes open the oven door gently and press the tops of the cakes, if they feel springy they are cooked, if not pop them back in to bake a little longer and try again after a further 5 minutes or so.

Remove from the oven and carefully tip out onto a wire cooling rack leaving them to become cold.

In a small bowl, make the topping by sifting the icing sugar and adding enough egg white to form a stiff mixture as it will need to hold its shape when being piped.

When the cakes are completely cold, stand them upright onto a serving plate and pipe a ring of icing around the outer edge of the top of the cakes. Finally carefully spoon a little of the red jam into the centre of the icing ring. Your cakes are now ready to eat on 5th February, although I don't suppose anyone will mind if you eat them simply when you fancy.

COCONUT CAKE

INDIA

Coconut is used in many Indian dishes, both sweet and savoury. The coconut cake, is not dissimilar in appearance to coconut ice, a popular sweet in many parts of the world, but this recipe uses butter, making it really rather different.

175g/6oz butter
400g/14oz desiccated coconut
275ml/10fl oz condensed milk

Melt the butter slowly in a heavy bottomed, medium saucepan. Add the coconut, stirring constantly with a wooden spoon. Finally stir in the condensed milk and cook for about 10 minutes continuing to stir. The mixture will thicken.

Pour into a well buttered baking tin approximately 20x25cm/8x10in, and allow to set and become completely cold before cutting into dainty squares. Excellent for afternoon tea.

PUMPKIN AND CREAM CHEESE MUFFINS

NEW ZEALAND   *MAKES 12*

When friends Foster and Jackie Edwards went to New Zealand for several weeks they returned with cake recipes for me from several New Zealand bakers. This is one of their discoveries.

120g/4oz softened butter
120g/4oz soft pale brown sugar
3 tablespoons molasses
1 egg, lightly beaten
275g/10oz cooked, mashed pumpkin

275g/10oz self-raising flour
1 teaspoon bicarbonate of soda
1 teaspoon ground cinnamon
1 teaspoon ground ginger
225g/8oz cream cheese

Preheat the oven to 200°C/400°F/Gas Mark 6.

Using an electric hand mixer, cream the butter and sugar in a bowl until light and fluffy. Then mixing on the slowest speed, add the molasses and egg a little at a time followed by the pumpkin, flour, bicarbonate of soda, cinnamon and ginger.

Line a muffin tin with paper cases and half fill the muffin cases with the cake mixture, followed by a teaspoonful of the cream cheese finally topping the cases with more of the mix.

Fill all the muffin cases and bake in the centre of the oven for about 15 minutes or until browned and firm to the touch when pressed lightly in the centre.

OHAGI WAGASHI

JAPAN   *Makes 12*

Dr Sheena Bradley, who works with my husband, recently flew to Japan for her son's wedding and kindly found time to look for Japanese cakes. Fortunately, her son's father-in-law is a chef who elaborated on the apparent absence of cakes in Japan, in particular celebration cakes. He explained that confectionery and sweets take their place within a meal, being a small part of the happy story a meal would tell. The designs are always imaginative, often changing with the seasons, so every cake is beautifully presented with birds, flowers, leaves and blossom. Seasons and harmony are always carefully reflected both in the food eaten and its visual appeal.

Little or no dairy produce is ever used in Japanese cakes but sweet adzuki bean paste features in the small but exquisite range of handmade Japanese cakes as does glutinous rice. Simple ingredients, rice and adzuki paste, prove I believe, the astonishing ingenuity shown by Japanese chefs and the following recipe is a good example.

225g/8oz Japanese glutinous rice (short grain pudding rice)
500g/16oz tinned, cooked adzuki beans
150g/5oz caster sugar

30cm/12in square of muslin or cheesecloth

Rinse the rice before putting into a saucepan; add just enough water to cover. Bring to the boil before reducing to a steady simmer. When the rice is soft (about 20 minutes) drain and allow to cool. Form the rice into 12 evenly sized balls and set aside.

In another saucepan empty the can of adzuki beans together with their liquid, slowly bringing to boiling point before adding the sugar and stirring well. Allow the beans to simmer until the liquid has almost cooked away before removing from the heat and mashing to form a smooth paste.

Dampen the piece of muslin or cheesecloth and spread out onto a work surface and spoon 2 1/2 tablespoons of the red bean paste into the centre, and using the back of the spoon gently spread and flatten the mixture into a circle large enough to enfold a rice ball. Place a rice ball into the centre and with the help of the damp cloth, lift and press the paste to form an outer layer. Repeat until the rice balls have all been covered with an outer layer of adzuki paste. Place each Ohagi onto a plate – with the joins underneath and out of sight. Decorate the plate with a small bunch of seasonal flowers or leaves, and if liked place a petal on top of each cake.

KOEKSISTERS

SOUTH AFRICA   *Makes 8*

My friend Pamela Bradshaw was born in South Africa and recently married a handsome young man from our village, so her knowledge of the cakes of her homeland was genuinely very close to hand and also my Pop had lived there for many years. So why is this relevant? It is relevant, because whoever I asked, where ever I asked Koeksisters (pronounced 'cook-sisters') fritters were always the first cakes which came up in conversation, proving their popularity. From the Dutch word *koekje*, the diminutive of *koek* meaning cake. They are syrup-coated doughnuts with twisted or plaited deep fried dough. Immediately after frying, these decorative, little fritters are drained for a moment before being plunged into an ice-cold syrup, which forms their crisp outer shell.

Syrup
700g/1lb 8oz granulated sugar
300ml/1/2 pint water
Grated rind of a lemon
1 cinnamon stick

450g/1lb self-raising flour
2 teaspoons baking powder
125g/5oz firm butter
2 eggs, lightly beaten
About 250ml/8fl oz milk

Corn oil for frying

To ensure crisp sweet fritters, prepare the syrup the day before and allow to cool overnight in the fridge.

To make the syrup, measure the sugar and water into a medium sized saucepan, bring to the boil and stir until the sugar has dissolved. Add the lemon rind and cinnamon and boil briskly for about 5 minutes. Remove the saucepan from the heat and leave to become completely cold before pouring the syrup into a bowl and placing in the refrigerator until needed.

The following day, sift the flour and baking powder into a bowl. Grate the butter and stir into the flour before adding the eggs and approximately half the milk. Pull the ingredients together, using your hands, and form the dough into a ball. Knead thoroughly for several minutes, adding more milk if necessary, to ensure a firm not sticky dough. Cover the bowl with a clean cloth and place in the refrigerator for about an hour.

On a lightly floured surface, roll out the dough and cut into strips about 10cm/4in long and 4cm/11/2in wide. Cut each strip into three, but leave them intact at the top end of each section, finally plait each one to form a plaited cake, pinching the bottom ends to secure.

Heat the cooking oil until it is hot and lightly smoking, and lower the Koeksisters two or three at a time into the oil. Turn them over after 2-3 minutes; fry them until pale golden brown, they will need no longer than 4-5 minutes to cook.

Using a slotted spoon lift the cakes from the oil and plunge immediately into the cold syrup, making sure they are completely covered, before lifting out and leaving to drain on a rack.

Tip: Use only half of the syrup at a time, leaving the other half in the refrigerator, swapping them around so that they remain really cold. Unless the syrup is really cold the Koeksisters will not be crisp.

DUCKANOO CAKES

CARIBBEAN   *Makes 12*

It is generally agreed that Duckanoo Cakes, also known as Conkies, originally came from West Africa where they were made to be eaten during the old British colonial celebration of Guy Fawkes Day on November 5th. They are traditionally wrapped in plantain or banana leaves before steaming but you can cook them in little foil parcels – unless of course, you have access to banana or plantain leaves.

350g/12oz grated fresh coconut
600ml/1 pint milk
450g/1lb finely milled cornmeal
50g/2oz currants
50g/2oz sultanas
50g/2oz raisins

175g/6oz soft pale brown sugar
50g/2oz melted butter
1/2 teaspoon ground cinnamon
1/2 teaspoon ground nutmeg
1/4 teaspoon ground cloves
1 teaspoon vanilla extract

Measure the grated coconut and milk into a food processor and whiz until smooth. Measure the cornmeal into a large bowl and add the coconut liquid, while stirring. Add all the other ingredients and stir until thoroughly mixed.

Using some squares of tin foil approximately 15x15cm/6x6in put about a tablespoonful of the cake mixture into the centre of each, folding them to form a parcel. Do make sure that they will be waterproof by folding the edges tightly. Continue until all the mixture is used.

Half fill a large saucepan with water and bring to the boil. Gently drop in all the parcels and replace the lid. Simmer gently for about an hour, before carefully unwrapping the cakes and leaving them on a wire rack to cool.

CHOCOLATE BROWNIES

USA   *Makes 12*

Somehow I find it impossible to think about American cakes without dwelling on chocolate brownies. Moist and gooey in the middle, the quickest way to spoil them is to over cook them, they really are meant to be soft in the centre.

Various things can be added to the mixture to make them a little different, chocolate chips or chopped nuts being the favourites.

275g/10oz plain chocolate   1 teaspoon vanilla extract
225g/8oz butter   115g/4oz self-raising flour
3 large eggs   115g/4oz chopped pecan nuts
225g/8oz soft pale brown sugar   115g/4oz plain chocolate chips

Preheat the oven to 180°C/350°F/Gas Mark 4.

Gently melt the chocolate and butter together in a small bowl, over a saucepan of hot water. Set aside to cool.

In a separate bowl, whisk together the eggs, sugar and vanilla before stirring in the chocolate, butter mixture.

Gently fold the flour, pecan nuts and chocolate chips into the brownie mixture, stir and pour into a greased oblong tin, 30x20cm/12x8in.

Bake in the centre of the oven for about 35-40 minutes. The top will have formed a sugary crust. Leave to cool in the tin and when cold cut into squares, using a sharp knife.

PASTÉIS DE NATA / CUSTARD TARTS

PORTUGAL   *Makes 12*

These little custard tarts are among the most popular sweet treats in Portugal. Although not entirely simple to make – they do need care – they are well worth the time taken.

275g/10oz puff pastry
50g/2oz caster sugar
1 teaspoon ground nutmeg
1 teaspoon ground cinnamon
1 egg yolk, beaten

Custard
5 large eggs, beaten
6 tablespoons clear honey
1 teaspoon vanilla extract
Zest of 1 orange
600ml/1 pint double cream

Preheat the oven to 200°C/400°F/Gas Mark 6.

On a lightly floured surface, roll out the pastry thinly. Sprinkle the surface evenly with the sugar, nutmeg and cinnamon. Fold the pastry in half and roll out again, thinly.

Using a cutter, stamp out 12 rounds and press them into a 12 hole non-stick tart tin. Prick the base of the pastry cases and line with a small piece of greaseproof or foil, add a few baking beans to each and bake blind in the oven for 10 minutes. Remove the foil and beans, brush lightly with the beaten egg yolk and return to the oven for 2-3 minutes. This will prevent the pastry cases from becoming soggy when filled with the custard mixture. Leave the cases in the baking tray and allow to cool.

Meanwhile measure the eggs, honey, vanilla, zest and double cream into a saucepan and stirring constantly, cook gently until it thickens. Be very careful not to allow the mixture to burn.

If necessary, strain the filling before pouring it equally into the pastry cases. Leave them to set as the mixture cools.

If you like you may top them with a little caramel. In a small saucepan bring 6 tablespoons caster sugar and 3 tablespoons water to the boil and cook until it thickens and becomes golden brown. Pour a little over each tart and allow it to set before serving.

MERINGUES

Makes 5

It is difficult to know to which country to attribute meringues, but they are certainly widely baked in France and were probably taken to other countries including England, during the time when having a French chef was a status symbol, as the French were seen as true culinary professionals.

Easy to make but patience is required as meringues must be cooked, or perhaps dried-out is a better term, very slowly in order that they are beautifully crisp. These well loved small cakes can be finished in many ways, but the most popular is to sandwich two together with freshly whipped cream.

2 egg whites
115g/4oz caster sugar

150ml/1/4 pint double cream

Preheat the oven to 120°C/250°F/Gas Mark 1/2.

Using an electric hand mixer, whisk the egg whites in a clean bowl, until stiff. Add half the sugar and whisk again until the egg whites are standing in peaks.

Gently fold in the remaining sugar, using a large metal spoon. Put the meringue mixture into a large piping bag, with a suitable nozzle and pipe the meringue mixture onto a very lightly greased baking tray, lined with greaseproof paper, in your preferred size.

Bake the meringues in the centre of the very cool oven for 2 or 3 hours, the time taken will vary, until the meringues are firm and dry.

Allow the cakes to cool before sandwiching them together in pairs with whipped double cream.

CUP CAKES

USA   *Makes 12*

I had never really given much thought as to why Cup Cakes were so called, but I have been reliably informed that it was because the ingredients were always measured in 'cups'.

Recipes for these popular cakes are prolific but I felt that in loyalty to my favourite, I would bake the chocolate variety and hope that you will be happy to make a similar batch.

115g/4oz butter
115g/4oz soft pale brown sugar
2 large eggs, separated
115g/4oz self-raising flour
1/2 teaspoon baking powder
1 tablespoon milk

Butter icing
115g/4oz unsalted butter
115g/4oz sifted icing sugar

Preheat the oven to 180°C/350°F/Gas Mark 4.

Using an electric hand mixer, cream the butter and sugar together in a large bowl until light and fluffy. On a low speed add the egg yolks, flour, baking powder and milk and mix until well blended.

In a separate bowl, whisk the egg whites until stiff and using a metal tablespoon, gently fold them into the cake mixture.

Spoon an equal amount of the cup cake mixture into a 12 hole muffin tin lined with greaseproof paper cases, filling each case two-thirds full. Bake in the centre of the oven for about 15-20 minutes or until the cakes feel springy when pressed gently in the middle.

Leave them for 5 minutes before lifting them out of the tin and onto a cooling rack.

Cream the butter and icing sugar together until soft and smooth, before adding colouring if liked.

LAMINGTONS

AUSTRALIA *Makes 24*

It would be very difficult to think of Australian cakes without Lamingtons appearing very near the top of the list. Undoubtedly named after Baron Lamington, who was the Governor of Queensland from 1895 until 1901, these little sponge squares are coated with a chocolate icing and tossed in coconut and are traditionally served on every occasion where cakes form the centrepiece.

Sponge Base
175g/6oz butter
175g/6oz caster sugar
175g/6oz self-raising flour
3 large eggs, lightly beaten

Chocolate Icing
500g/1lb icing sugar
15g/1/2oz butter
4 tablespoons cocoa
Approximately 100ml/4fl oz boiling water

Topping
250g/8oz desiccated coconut

Preheat the oven to 180°C/350°F/Gas Mark 4.

Cream the butter and sugar until pale and fluffy before adding the flour and eggs, a little at a time. When fully incorporated spoon the sponge mixture into a greased and lined 20x30cm/8x12in cake tin, smoothing the top of the mixture gently.

Bake for about 30 minutes until risen, golden brown and springy to touch. Remove from the oven and allow to become completely cold in its tin.

Place a heatproof bowl over a saucepan of simmering water. Measure the icing sugar, butter, cocoa and water into the bowl and stir quickly until the icing becomes smooth and shiny. Remove from the heat.

Cut the cold sponge into even-sized squares about 6x6cm/2x2in. Measure the coconut into a second bowl and then toss the little sponge cakes firstly into the chocolate icing and then into the coconut, placing the finished cakes onto a rack to dry.

When the coating is set, they are ready to enjoy.

OLIEBOLLEN

HOLLAND   *Makes 15*

While researching for this book a rather insignificant little dough cake kept pleading for attention. Varying in shape, sometimes with a topping, or just lashings of sugar, occasionally with a filling of jam or perhaps chocolate, or maybe no filling at all or just a hole, yet somehow over the centuries doughnuts keep bobbing up. And now I have to admit that I love them.

100ml/4fl oz lukewarm water
25g/1oz fresh yeast
1 teaspoon caster sugar
450g/1lb strong white bread flour
1 egg, lightly beaten
50g/2oz caster sugar
425ml/15fl oz lukewarm milk
75g/3oz sultanas

50g/2oz mixed chopped peel
50g/2oz currants

Topping
100g/4oz icing sugar
1 teaspoon ground cinnamon

Pour the water into a small jug and add the yeast and sugar. Stir thoroughly before setting aside to froth.

In a large bowl sift the flour, making a dip in the centre. Add the egg, sugar, yeast mixture and lukewarm milk, mixing thoroughly. Cover with a damp tea towel and set aside to double in size. After about 1 hour, add the dried fruit and peel to the dough, mixing thoroughly. Set aside for a further 45 minutes or until the dough doubles in volume.

Finally, heat the oil in a deep pan fryer to approximately 180°C/350°F before dropping tablespoons of the mixture into the oil. It is better to cook only 3 or 4 at a time so that you have no problem turning the Oliebollen over after they begin to brown – about 4 minutes on each side is about right. Using a slotted spoon, scoop the cooked cakes onto a plate, covered with kitchen roll, to help drain off any excess oil. Repeat until all the dough is used.

Finally dust with icing sugar and a little cinnamon to taste.

MUFFINS

USA   *Makes 12*

Almost every American bakery or coffee shop will have an enormous variety of muffins piled on trays. Eaten while still warm for breakfast, they are great with coffee or hot chocolate.

Perhaps the biggest problem with muffins is deciding which flavour to choose and I have had similar problems selecting which recipe to give, so I have opted for simple raisin and cinnamon muffins, which are great with butter and jam. Muffins are traditionally freshly baked each day, perhaps because the previous day's muffins have always been eaten!

275g/10oz self-raising flour
1 teaspoon baking powder
1 teaspoon ground cinnamon
75g/3oz butter
75g/3oz soft pale brown sugar

115g/4oz raisins
2 eggs, lightly beaten
250ml/8fl oz buttermilk

Preheat the oven to 200°C/400°F/Gas Mark 6.

Sift the flour into a large bowl, together with the baking powder and cinnamon. Rub the butter into the flour, using your fingertips and stir in the sugar and raisins.

Pour in the beaten eggs and buttermilk, stirring constantly. If the mixture is a little lumpy that does not matter at all.

Spoon the muffin mixture equally into a 12 hole muffin tin lined with paper cases and put them straight into the centre of the preheated oven. Bake for about 20 minutes or until golden brown and firm to touch. Remove from the muffin tin onto a cooling rack and serve while still warm.

ANZAC BISCUITS

NEW ZEALAND

Though not strictly speaking cakes, it would be very difficult to write this book without including these very significant biscuits.

ANZAC is an acronym for Australia and New Zealand Army Corps and ANZAC day, April 25th, is a national holiday in New Zealand when the troops who fell on the battlefields are remembered.

Now produced commercially, plenty of families still prefer to bake them at home because of their symbolic significance of remembrance.

115g/4oz butter	115g/4oz plain flour
1 tablespoon golden syrup	175g/6oz soft pale brown sugar
1/2 teaspoon baking soda	175g/6oz desiccated coconut
2 tablespoons boiling water	175g/6oz rolled oats

Preheat the oven to 180°C/350°F/Gas Mark 4.

Melt the butter and syrup gently in a small saucepan.

Dissolve the baking soda in the boiling water and stir into the butter and syrup mixture.

In a large bowl, stir together the flour, sugar, coconut and oats. Make a well in the centre and stir in the butter mixture. When thoroughly combined, place dessertspoonfuls onto a well greased baking tray and place in the centre of the preheated oven to bake. Check after about 15 minutes by which time they will be golden brown and crisp.

After 2 or 3 minutes, remove carefully from the baking tray and transfer onto the wire cooling rack.

AWWAMAAT

LEBANON

So many cakes and pastries in the Middle East are gloriously sticky, having been either dipped in syrup or having had syrup gently poured over them. The Awwamaat doughnuts are no exception and are traditionally baked to celebrate the baptism of Jesus Christ.

700g/1 1/2lbs plain flour	**Syrup**
1 teaspoon baking soda	350g/12oz granulated sugar
600ml/1 pint plain yogurt	600ml/1 pint water
	1 tablespoon lemon juice
	2 tablespoons orange flower water

Sift the flour and baking soda into a large bowl and add the yogurt. Stir with a pallet knife until it is gathered together so it can be transferred onto a lightly floured work surface. Knead well until the dough is smooth.

Heat a saucepan one third filled with corn oil or olive oil, until a tiny piece of the dough, dropped into the oil, immediately rises to the surface and begins to brown.

Drop two or three dessertspoonfuls of the dough into the oil, taking them out using a slotted spoon, as soon as they rise to the top. Put them onto some kitchen roll to allow them to drain.

When all the doughnuts are fried, put all the ingredients for the syrup into a small saucepan and bring to the boil, allow to simmer for about 10 minutes before briefly dipping the cakes into the syrup.

SUFGANIOT or PONCHKES / HANNUKAH DOUGHNUTS

ISRAEL   *Makes 8*

These are baked to celebrate Hannukah 'The Festival of Lights', a Jewish remembrance day dating back to before Christ when an oil lamp, with only enough lamp fuel for one day remained alight for eight days and nights. Prepared in much the same way as other doughnuts, the symbolism for this cake at Hannukah is that they are fried in oil.

150ml/5fl oz tepid water
14g/1/2 oz dried yeast
1 teaspoon sugar
700g/11/2lbs plain flour
50g/2oz caster sugar
3 large eggs
115g/4oz softened butter

1 teaspoon vanilla extract

Filling
Strawberry preserve

Icing sugar to dust

Pour the water into a small bowl and add the yeast and sugar. Set aside in a warm place.

Sift the flour into a large bowl, make a well in the centre and add the sugar, eggs, butter and vanilla extract; using a hand mixer on slow speed, mix together thoroughly. Add the yeast and using your hands, work the dough into a ball, before lifting onto a floured surface and kneading for about 5 to 10 minutes until the dough is smooth and spongy. Wash and grease the bowl before lifting the dough back in, covering and setting aside to double in size, this will take at least one hour.

Once the dough has risen, roll it out on a lightly floured surface and using a cutter, press out as many 7.5cm/3in circles of dough as possible.

Drop a teaspoonful of the preserve into the centre of half of the circles of dough. Lightly wet the outer edges and place a second dough circle on top, pressing the edges of the doughnuts together. Cover the cakes with a clean tea towel and leave for about 30 minutes to rise.

Meanwhile in a fairly large saucepan, pour enough olive or corn oil in which to fry the doughnuts, about a third full is perfect.

When the doughnuts have risen, heat the oil until it just begins to smoke and a small piece of dough dropped into the oil will immediately rise to the surface, bubbling.

Begin frying the doughnuts, two at a time, turning them over carefully with a slotted spoon. They will cook very quickly and as soon as they are golden brown on both sides, lift them out onto a sheet of absorbent kitchen roll and allow them to cool completely before eating as the jam in the centre will be very hot and could burn your mouth.

CHURROS

SPAIN   *Makes 5-6*

I feel compelled to say that few Spaniards would actually cook these little cakes themselves since every corner café, every market place has stalls with deep frying pans from which they produce hot, freshly cooked Churros for dunking in a hot chocolate drink - more of that later. The dough is piped from a large bag fitted with a star nozzle, giving these doughnuts their characteristic appearance, before cooking for a few minutes in hot oil, lifting out and tossing in caster sugar and cinnamon.

The Spanish Conquistadors brought chocolate from Mexico in the 16th century and it is still held in great esteem. The chocolate drink, which is served with Churros, is made by combining solid chocolate with milk in a small saucepan, sugar to taste, before whisking a little to ensure the chocolate has melted before pouring into a large cup ready for dunking.

50g/2oz butter	**Topping**
175g/6oz plain white flour	115g/4oz caster sugar
1 teaspoon caster sugar	1 teaspoon ground cinnamon
150ml/1/4 pint water	
2 lightly beaten eggs	

Prepare the topping by mixing the sugar and cinnamon together on a large plate. Set aside.

Measure the butter, flour, sugar and water into a medium saucepan and heat slowly, while stirring constantly with a wooden spoon. Cook for a few minutes until the mixture forms a ball. Take from the heat and tip the dough into a bowl. Using a hand held mixer on low speed, add the lightly beaten eggs, a little at a time, until fully incorporated. The dough should be quite firm.

Heat the oil in a deep pan fryer to about 180°C/350°F. Using a large piping bag fitted with a star nozzle about 5mm/1/4in diameter, fill with some of the mixture and squeezing gently (I find it best to hold the bag in your left hand and kitchen scissors in your right) cut lengths of mixture, about 9cm/3-4in long, carefully allowing them to drop into the oil. Work quite quickly, cooking a few at a time, as each Churros will take only about 4 minutes to cook. Remove them from the oil with a slotted spoon allowing them to drain for a moment before tossing them in the sugar and cinnamon.

Best eaten while warm and of course, only after dunking in the hot chocolate!

DOUGHNUTS

MOROCCO   *Makes 18-20*

While I am not suggesting you try to replicate the vast drums of boiling cooking oil, which are found on roadsides and in the souks of Morocco, these doughnuts are so good that it is well worthwhile searching for a smaller receptacle in which to deep fry them.

2 teaspoons dried yeast	400g/14oz plain flour
1 teaspoon caster sugar	1 lightly beaten egg
275ml/10fl oz lukewarm water	
	Caster sugar

Place the yeast and sugar into a small bowl and adding a little of the water, stir until they have dissolved. Set aside in a warm room for about 15 minutes, to become frothy.

Sift the flour into a larger mixing bowl and making a well in the centre, stir in the yeast, beaten egg and the remaining water, stirring with a pallet knife until it forms a ball. Lift the dough onto a lightly floured surface and knead for 5 to 10 minutes until it becomes smooth and springy. Place the dough in a clean lightly oiled bowl, cover with a cloth and leave in a warm room to double in size, which will take about an hour. Turn out onto a floured worktop and divide the dough into 18-20 pieces of equal size. Roll each piece into a ball and finish by making a hole in the centre with your finger.

Fill a large saucepan a third full with fresh cooking oil. Heat the oil to 180°C/350°F. Gently lower two or three doughnuts into the hot oil, turning them over with a spatula after about 2 or 3 minutes. Cook for about 5 minutes or until golden brown.

Finally using a slotted spoon gently lift them onto a plate lined with some kitchen roll and allow to drain before rolling them in caster sugar.

INUIT BANNOCK DOUGHNUTS

CANADA

Makes 5-6

I discovered that in 1992 the Inuit Circumpolar Conference served 'Eskimo Doughnuts' made from bannock dough. In its simplest form the dough would have been flour, fat and salt, which was often wrapped around a stick and cooked over an open fire; they were 'dampers', but with the addition of butter and sugar the dough was enriched to become a doughnut, which I understand were and still are extremely popular amongst the Inuit communities.

200g/7oz plain flour	25g/1oz melted butter
2 teaspoons baking powder	Water to mix
Pinch of salt	
2 tablespoons sugar	Sugar to finish

Sift the flour and baking powder into a bowl and add the pinch of salt. Stir in the sugar and the melted butter, finally adding just enough water to form soft but not sticky dough.

Roll into balls about 5cm/2in in diameter and flatten slightly before pressing a hole through the centre of each doughnut, forming a ring.

Using a deep fat fryer, heat oil until just smoking and cook two or three of the doughnut rings at a time, turning each with a slotted spoon until golden brown and puffy. This will only take 4 or 5 minutes. Lift from the oil and drain on paper towels for a moment or two, before dipping each cake into the sugar to coat them.

Set them aside to cool before eating but they are best eaten the same day.

KRAPFEN

Makes 6

When reading a detailed article on Austrian doughnuts I counted no less than 21 different varieties and fascinatingly there are specific days of the year on which they are baked.

There are celebrations at which doughnuts always make an appearance and the varieties of doughnut which may be baked on those occasions is specified, all with a reason for their inclusion – indeed it appears that the only time *Krapfen* never appear is at funerals. In Germany there are similar ones which have raspberry jam in the centre but I have also seen them covered with melted chocolate and filled with a custard cream filling. They are called *Pfannkuchen* or *Oder Krapfen* (or Bismarck after the Prussian statesman who was known to have a soft spot for them).

Two packets of 7g/1/4oz instant yeast
1 teaspoon caster sugar
2 tablespoons lukewarm water
300ml/1/2 pint lukewarm milk
60g/21/2 oz butter
50g/2oz sugar
2 eggs, lightly beaten

560g/1lb 4oz plain flour

Filling
1 jar apricot (or raspberry) conserve
1 egg, lightly beaten
Caster sugar

Stir the yeast, caster sugar and water together in a jug and set it aside to froth. Combine the milk, butter and sugar in a small saucepan and warm gently, stirring until the butter and sugar have melted before pouring onto the yeast mixture.

Sift the flour into a large bowl making a well in the centre, pour in the yeast mixture and stir until it forms a ball. Turn the dough onto a floured worktop and knead the dough for about 5 minutes until it forms a smooth ball. Lift into a clean bowl, cover with a damp cloth and set aside in a warm place to double in size, this usually takes about 1 hour.

Turn the dough onto a well floured surface and knead for a couple of minutes before rolling out to about 2cm/3/4in thick. Using a round 5cm/2in cutter, press out as many doughnut rounds as possible. Finally, place a spoonful of the apricot jam into the centre of a round; brush the edges with a little egg before topping it with a second round, pressing the edges of each doughnut together. Set aside for about 20 minutes to allow them to rise again.

Deep fry them in corn oil, two or three at a time, turning them over as soon as they become nicely browned. Lift them out with a slotted spoon, allowing the Krapfen to drain before tossing in caster sugar.

MALASSADAS

Makes 24

Portuguese immigrants began arriving in Hawaii during the mid 1800s looking for work and brought with them their traditions and food recipes. One of the most popular dishes they introduced was the doughnut Malassadas, which over a period of time became so popular, that even today the bakers compete for recognition as 'the best doughnut baker in Hawaii'. There are even sign posts erected to direct both tourists and the Hawaiians to the Malassadas baker's shops.

The Portuguese eat them on Shrove Tuesday as is their tradition, but the other residents of the Hawaiian Islands try to find any good reason to involve them in a celebration or carnival, simply because they are delicious to eat.

4 teaspoons active dried yeast	6 large eggs
1 teaspoon sugar	300ml/1/2 pint milk
300ml/1/2 pint warm water	
900g/2lbs plain flour	**Decoration**
125g/4oz caster sugar	Sugar and cinnamon
60g/2oz melted butter	

Mix the yeast, sugar and lukewarm water together in a small jug. Set aside to begin to froth.

Measure the flour and sugar into a large bowl and stir before adding the melted butter, lightly beaten eggs and the milk. Stir again before adding the jug of yeast mix. Using your hands, knead the dough until it comes together before turning onto a lightly floured surface and kneading for about 10 minutes until the mixture becomes smooth and spongy. Put the dough back into the clean and lightly oiled bowl, cover and leave in a warm place to rise. After about 45 minutes, turn out onto a lightly floured surface and knead briefly before dividing into evenly sized pieces and rolling into balls about 6cm/21/2in in diameter.

Meanwhile fill a medium sized saucepan about a third full of corn oil and heat slowly until the oil begins to smoke a little taking care, drop a small piece of dough into the oil, when after spluttering it will rise to the surface quite quickly. This means that the oil is hot enough. Using a slotted spoon, lower the balls of dough into the oil, about 2 or 3 at a time, turning them over occasionally until they are golden brown. Using the spoon, lift them from the pan and place on a little kitchen roll to drain.

Mix the caster sugar and ground cinnamon together on a plate and roll each doughnut around until they are evenly covered. Place onto a clean plate and leave to cool slightly before eating.

YEAST CAKES

It isn't always easy to differentiate between bread and cakes, particularly when the cakes or tea breads are both baked with yeast, but generally speaking bread is savoury and raised with yeast and water, while the tea breads or yeast cakes are enriched with butter, often eggs and always milk, giving them a more crumbly texture and cake-like taste. Some dried fruits and spices are generally added to sweet tea breads and any other ingredients will differ between countries; Spanish Pestinos or Italian Panettone are perfect examples.

Local recipes reflect local ingredients and customs with perhaps a tea bread being eaten on a certain day, or at a certain time of the year. Christstollen, mentioned in German records as far back as the 12th century, are very much part of the tradition of yeast cakes, representing the Holy Child in swaddling clothes. The Bread of the Dead is a cake traditionally eaten on All Souls Day, throughout Mexico.

One thing which struck me, as I looked at the yeast cake recipes, was how often they were baked in a certain mould, giving them their characteristic shape, or how they might be decorated in a particular way. An excellent example is the Russian Kulitch, which is always baked in a tall cylindrical mould and decorated with drizzled icing and a flower or candle on the top.

I do hope you will want to bake some of the cakes in this section, even if you do have to be imaginative when looking for a suitable cake tin or cake decoration.

BABA AU RHUM /RUM BABA

Makes 6-7 cakes

Cakes often have such interesting backgrounds that it can be a problem sorting the truth from the fairytales and let's face it sometimes the fairytales can be far more interesting.

During the 18th century the Polish King Stanislas Lecsczinski, Duke of Lorraine, was living in exile in France, as his daughter was married to the French King Louis XV. Stanislas found the French cake Kugelhopf very dry, so imagine his delight when having spilt his glass of rum over a slice, found it so vastly improved that he asked his chef to make it in that way in future. The Duke's hero was Ali Baba from the Arabian Nights, so a new cake with a new name was born.

15g/¹/₂oz fresh yeast	60g/2oz currants
30g/1oz caster sugar	
150ml/¹/₄ pint lukewarm milk	**Syrup**
225g/8oz plain flour	Grated zest of a lemon
3 large eggs	300ml/¹/₂ pint water
125g/4oz melted butter	225g/8oz sugar
2 tablespoons rum	3 tablespoons rum

You will need individual (11.5cm/4¹/₂in) baby savarin (rum baba) moulds for this recipe.

Preheat the oven to 200°C/400°F/Gas Mark 6. Cream the yeast and sugar, add the milk, stir and set aside in a warm place until frothy.

Sift the flour into a large bowl making a dip in the centre. Using an electric mixer, pour the yeast mix into the flour, together with the eggs, melted butter and rum. It is better to do this a little at a time, mixing constantly. Beat on a low speed until the dough becomes smooth and shiny, add the currants and mix again, just enough to incorporate them into the dough. Cover the bowl with a damp cloth and leave in a warm place to double in size – about 1 hour.

Generously butter the Baba cake tins and put them onto a large baking sheet.

Lift the dough onto a lightly floured surface and knead for a couple of minutes before dividing the dough into the required number of portions, put each portion of dough into a buttered tin and smooth them down a little with your fingers. Put the little Baba tins back onto the baking tray and leave in a warm place. When the dough has reached the top of the tins place them into the oven and bake for about 15 minutes until golden brown, they should feel firm to the touch. Turn out onto a cooling rack and leave to become almost cold. If reluctant to leave their tins, run a knife gently around each cake.

Meanwhile put the lemon, water and sugar into a small saucepan, bring to the boil and simmer for about 10 minutes, until a light syrup forms. Set aside to cool a little. Place the Babas onto a serving plate and spoon the rum syrup over each cake. Finish with generous swirls of double cream and one or two pieces of fresh fruit.

PESTINOS

SPAIN   *Makes approx 24*

Kate, who bakes alongside me here at Church Farmhouse, recently visited the lovely town of Rota in the Bay of Cadiz on the south west coast of Spain. Even on holiday such obsessive cake makers are unable to switch off and so it was no surprise that she brought back recipes and some of the ingredients for *Pestinos*, one of the most popular traditional Christmas cakes in that region. It was the enchantingly named Aurora Luna, one of the residents of Rota, who told Kate the history of these little cakes.

Traditionally a family affair, the ladies gather to prepare all the ingredients, kneading by hand before rolling the dough fairly thinly and cutting it into squares, finally pulling two of the corners into the middle to form a horn shape. Then in between much laughter and merriment they are fried to a golden brown before being drizzled with honey and allowed to cool. After which the cakes are shared between family members and taken to their respective homes for eating during the festivities.

I also came across a reference to *Pestinos* in a book I was reading and it appears that the nuns in Seville cut them into equal sized pieces of dough, form them into little log shapes, and roll them in sesame seeds. Another recipe suggests using fresh orange juice instead of the white wine, adding ground almonds and replacing the lemon peel with a mixture of orange and lemon peel. Clearly like a lot of baking, these little cakes vary slightly in different areas of Spain.

275ml/10fl oz olive oil	2 teaspoons dried yeast
Peel of one lemon	250ml/9fl oz Anise (aniseed flavour liquor)
1 teaspoon green anise spice	250ml/9fl oz white wine
1.5kg/3lbs plain flour	150ml/1/4 pint Muscatel
Pinch of salt	Sesame seeds
1/2 teaspoon ground cloves	

Heat the oil in a small frying pan and gently fry the lemon peel for about 10 minutes to impart the flavour into the oil. Lift out the lemon peel and add the green anise to the oil in the pan allowing it to fry gently for about 5 minutes. Leaving the green anise in the oil remove the pan from the heat and set aside to cool.

Sift the flour into a large mixing bowl and make a well in the centre. Add the salt, ground cloves and the dried yeast, mixing thoroughly before adding the Anise liquor, white wine, sweet Muscatel and the cool oil. Work the ingredients into a dough and gently knead for a few minutes before putting them into a clean bowl, covering with a clean cloth and leaving for about two hours to double in size.

Lift out the dough onto a lightly floured surface and knead well, rolling out thinly and cutting into 10cm/4in squares before forming them into the shape required. Fry in olive oil until golden brown.

In a small saucepan, simmer the honey and water and dip the fried Pestinos into the mixture while hot, setting aside on a cooling tray and sprinkling lightly with toasted sesame seeds.

PANETTONE

ITALY

It was our friends Kenneth and Ruth Wallace who first drew my attention to the charms of the Panettone. This cake or perhaps more accurately, sweet fruit loaf, is eaten as a Christmas cake in Italy, where it is beautifully boxed and ribboned. This festive speciality, now popular throughout the rest of Europe, is thought to have originated in Milan, (*pan del ton* meant luxury bread in Milanese dialect) where it was seen as a considerable treat, since sugar was available to only the very rich.

Kenneth, who is the great, great nephew of Isabella Beeton, and Ruth were trying to reproduce this traditional fruited cake but it was proving difficult to perfect. However all came good in the end and it is with pleasure that I detail Ruth's recipe.

450g/1lb strong flour
1 sachet dried yeast
300ml/1/2 pint tepid milk

150g/5oz butter
3 large egg yolks
75g/3oz caster sugar
Finely grated rind of 1 orange

100g/4oz pale golden sultanas
100g/4oz raisins
50g/2oz mixed peel
50g/2oz pine nuts
1 teaspoon mace

Topping
1 whole egg, beaten

You will require one 15cm/6in diameter new (or at least clean!) flowerpot lined with greaseproof paper.

Sift the flour into a large bowl, stir in the dried yeast and then add the tepid milk. Mix well with a pallet knife to form a soft ball before turning out onto a floured surface. Knead until smooth. Place into a clean bowl, cover with a cloth and leave in a warm place until double in size – usually takes about one hour.

Cut the butter into small pieces and together with the remaining ingredients add to the dough. Mixing with your hands, combine together thoroughly. Place the dough into the prepared flowerpot and leave in a warm place, checking now and again until it has risen to the top of the flowerpot. Preheat the oven to 200°C/400°F/Gas Mark 6.

Brush the top of the Panettone with the beaten egg and place in the centre of the oven. After 15 minutes turn down the oven to 180°C/350°F/Gas Mark 4 and continue to bake for a further 25-30 minutes or until the cake is golden brown and well risen. A skewer inserted into the centre of the cake should come out cleanly. If not, return to the oven and check again after another 10 minutes. Allow to cool a little before turning out onto a wire rack to become cold before eating – if you can wait.

CHRISTSTOLLEN

GERMANY

Serves 8-10 slices

Stollens are mentioned in German records as far back as the 12th century. They are very traditional Christmas cakes, symbolizing the Holy Child wrapped in swaddling clothes by the dough being rolled flat and then folded around fruit or almond paste.

Like most yeast baked cakes, preparation is a little time consuming but very enjoyable and you can take any lingering frustrations out on the dough while kneading.

400g/14oz strong bread flour	50g/2oz sultanas
50g/2oz soft pale brown sugar	50g/2oz currants
2 tablespoons dried yeast	50g/2oz raisins
150ml/1/4 pint milk	50g/2oz chopped glace cherries
115g/4oz butter	50g/2oz mixed citrus peel
1 tablespoon rum	50g/2oz chopped blanched almonds
1 egg, beaten	225g/8oz pale almond paste

Sift the flour into a large bowl and stir in the sugar and yeast. Gently heat the milk adding the butter and allow to melt before stirring in the rum.

Make a well in the centre of the flour and stir in the milk mixture together with the beaten egg. Mix thoroughly working it into a soft dough.

Flour a work surface and turn out the dough, kneading thoroughly until smooth and springy, about 10 minutes, before placing in a lightly greased bowl, cover with a clean tea towel and set aside in a warm place to rise. It will take about 1 hour for the dough to double in size.

Lightly flour your work surface and turn the risen dough out, kneading gently, add the fruits and almonds a little at a time, until evenly distributed throughout the dough. Roll the mixture into a rectangle about 23x18cm/9x7in and form the almond paste into a sausage about 15cm/6in in length, place it down the centre of the dough. Pull either side of the dough over the almond paste and carefully turn the dough over so that the join is underneath, before placing onto a greased baking sheet. Cover and leave to double in size, about 30-40 minutes. Preheat the oven to 200°C/ 400°F/Gas Mark 6.

Finally, bake in the oven for about 30 minutes until golden and firm to touch. Place on a wire rack to cool. When cold, dust generously with icing sugar before serving.

VASILOPITA / NEW YEAR CAKE

GREECE

Vasilopita is a compound Greek word which means the sweet 'bread of Basil' and it is baked as a New Year cake. There appear to be two quite different recipes for this cake, one based on an orange sweet bread dough and the other an orange, lemon and nut cake mixture. Because the recipes are equally delicious I have decided to include both, giving you the choice of which to bake; starting with the sweet bread cake variety. Both versions are cut and eaten at New Year and hidden within the cakes is a coin or charm which is supposed to bring the finder good luck for the coming year. Masticha (gum mastic) is an important ingredient in Greek festival breads and is also used as a spice. It grows extensively on the Greek island of Chios which is fabled as Homer's birthplace.

I sachet of active dried yeast
2 teaspoons caster sugar
190ml/6fl oz lukewarm milk
450g/1lb plain flour
1/2 teaspoon ground cinnamon
1/2 teaspoon ground nutmeg
1/2 teaspoon ground masticha
3 large eggs, lightly beaten
2 teaspoons finely grated zest and rind
    of an orange

150g/5oz caster sugar
115g/4oz butter, melted

Topping
I egg, lightly beaten
Flaked almonds

Charm of your choice

Empty the yeast into a small bowl with the sugar, adding a little of the milk. Stir and set aside in a warm place.

Measure the flour and spices into a large bowl, stir and make a well in the centre. Pour in the remaining milk, the lightly beaten eggs, orange zest and rind and sugar, together with the yeast mix. Stir well before gently pouring in the melted butter and then using your hands pull the dough into a ball before lifting it onto a lightly floured surface and kneading for about 8-10 minutes or until it is smooth and springy.

Put the dough into a clean, lightly greased bowl and cover with a cloth and set aside in a warm place to rise and double in size, which will take about 1 1/2 hours.

When the dough has risen, lift out and knead for a few minutes to take some of the air out before shaping it into a long sausage and lifting it onto a greased baking sheet. Pull the dough into a circle and using a little water to damp both ends of the dough, press them firmly together. Cover with a clean cloth and set aside for about an hour to double in size. Preheat the oven to 180°C/350°F/Gas Mark 4.

Finally wrap a coin in foil and press it into the underneath of the cake dough before glazing with the beaten egg and liberally sprinkling the flaked almonds.

Bake in the centre of the oven for about 45 minutes until the cake is golden brown and sounds hollow when tapped on the underside. Transfer the cooked Vasilopita onto a wire rack to cool. Best served on the day of baking.

POPPY SEED ROLL

POLAND

It would be extremely odd to find a Polish home without a Poppy Seed Roll to celebrate any occasion or festivity, or perhaps simply to enjoy, festivity or not. A delicious sweet yeast cake, filled with poppy seeds, raisins, ground almonds, chopped mixed peel and cinnamon.

350g/12oz strong plain flour
Pinch of salt
25g/1oz fresh yeast
50g/2oz caster sugar
120ml/4 fl oz lukewarm milk
1 large egg
50g/2oz melted butter
Zest of a lemon reserving the juice

Filling
125g/4oz poppy seeds
50g/2oz butter, melted
1 tablespoon honey
125g/4oz raisins
25g/1oz chopped mixed peel
50g/2oz ground almonds
1/2 teaspoon cinnamon

Icing
115g/4oz icing sugar
Juice of the lemon
Flaked almonds to decorate

Sift the flour and salt into a bowl, making a well in the centre. In a small bowl cream the fresh yeast and sugar, before adding the lukewarm milk, stir before setting it aside for a few minutes until it begins to froth. Add the melted butter, the zest of lemon and the lightly beaten egg to the flour, together with the yeast mix. Stir well before turning the dough onto a lightly floured surface and kneading well until the dough is smooth, soft and springy. Put the dough into a clean bowl and cover with a damp cloth, leave it in a warm place to double in size, which may take about an hour.

Meanwhile prepare the filling. Measure the poppy seeds into a small bowl, cover them with boiling water and allow to cool, before draining them through a fine sieve and returning them to the bowl. Add the melted butter, the honey, raisins, peel, almonds and cinnamon, stirring them together.

Turn the risen dough onto a lightly floured surface and knead gently before rolling it out into an oblong shape approximately 30x35cm/12x14in. Smooth the filling over the dough, coming to within 1cm/1/2in of the edge, before carefully rolling it up (rather like a Swiss roll) and lifting it onto a greased baking tray with the seam underneath. Set the cake aside to double in size. Heat the oven to 190°C/375°F/Gas Mark 5.

When the dough has risen, put the cake into the centre of the oven and bake for about 35 minutes or until golden brown.

Allow the cake to cool completely. Mix the icing sugar and lemon juice, adding a little at a time until smooth, but thick enough to spoon over the top of the cake. Finally sprinkle with a few flaked almonds.

PAN DE MUERTO /
BREAD OF THE DEAD

MEXICO
Makes about 12 portions

November 2nd is Dia de los Muertos or All Souls Day, when this simple but wonderfully aromatic orange bread cake is baked and eaten in remembrance of the dead. Not a very cheerful topic but nonetheless part of Mexican tradition.

150ml/5fl oz milk
50g/2oz butter
3 whole star anise

450g/1lb plain flour
1 1/4 teaspoons dried active yeast
50g/2oz pale soft brown sugar

2 eggs, lightly beaten
Zest of 2 oranges
2 tablespoons fresh orange juice
2 tablespoons Cointreau

Topping
A little icing sugar

Measure the milk into a small saucepan, add the butter and star anise. Heat gently until the butter melts and set aside to cool.

Sift the flour into a large bowl and add the dried yeast, sugar and orange zest, stirring thoroughly. Make a well in the centre.

Remove the star anise from the milk and pour the liquid into the flour, while stirring. Finally add the eggs, orange zest and juice and Cointreau. Beat the dough until all the ingredients are fully incorporated before lifting it carefully onto a lightly floured surface and kneading it until it becomes smooth and elastic.

Set aside in a clean bowl, covered with a cloth until it doubles in size. About 1-1 1/2 hours.

Knead the dough a little before placing it into a well greased 20cm/8in cake tin, a fluted tin would be perfect, and set it aside for a further 30 minutes to rise in the tin. Preheat the oven to 190°C/375°F/Gas Mark 5.

Bake the cake for about 40-50 minutes or until risen and golden brown. Remove from the oven and turn it onto a wire rack to cool. Lightly dust with icing sugar before serving.

BARMBRACK

IRELAND

The most famous of Irish cakes derives its name Barm from bairm or beorma meaning ale yeast and brack meaning speckles or spotted. Nobody would doubt that this fruited teacake lives up to its name perfectly. It is eaten sliced and buttered and may be baked either in a loaf tin or formed into a round and baked on a baking tray. Several varieties exist as bakers often have their favourite recipe and there is a connection with Halloween when 'charms' may be added to the mixture.

150g/5oz currants
150g/5oz raisins
50g/2oz sultanas
50g/2oz chopped mixed peel
300ml/1/2 pint cold strong tea

225g/8oz pale soft brown sugar
225g/8oz self raising flour
1 level teaspoon mixed spice
1 large egg, lightly beaten

Steep the currants, raisins and sultanas overnight in the cold tea.

The next day, preheat the oven to 180°C/350°F/Gas Mark 4 and grease and line a 900g/2lb loaf tin. Add all the remaining ingredients to the fruit, stirring thoroughly before spooning into the prepared tin.

Bake in the centre of the preheated oven for about 1 1/2 hours until risen and golden brown.

Turn out onto a wire cooling rack and allow to become cold, before serving sliced and buttered.

HERMAN CAKE

HAWAII

Herman Cake is clearly very popular in Hawaii though its history remains a mystery. Nonetheless it is well worth baking, even if the way in which it is put together may seem a little odd. A Herman by the way is a yeast starter, the recipe for which can be found on the following page.

225g/8oz soft pale brown sugar
1 teaspoon ground ginger
1 teaspoon ground cinnamon
50g/2oz chopped walnuts
50g/2oz chopped almonds
50g/2oz chopped macadamia nuts
50g/2oz fresh breadcrumbs

175g/6oz soft pale brown sugar
225g/8oz butter
2 eggs
450g/1lb flour
1 teaspoon baking powder
1 cup of Herman starter

225g/8oz crushed pineapple
2 tablespoons dark rum
125g/4oz butter, melted

Preheat the oven to 190°C/375°F/Gas Mark 5.

Mix together in a bowl the sugar, spices, nuts, and breadcrumbs.

In a separate bowl cream the sugar and butter with an electric hand mixer until pale and fluffy. Add the eggs slowly, beating constantly, until smooth. Add the flour, baking powder and Herman beating until fully incorporated.

Pour half the cake mixture into a 23x30cm/9x12in greased and lined square cake tin and sprinkle half of the sugar and nut mixture over the top, followed by the crushed pineapple. Spoon the remaining cake mixture over the top before sprinkling with the remaining sugar and nuts. Finally drizzle the cake with the rum and melted butter.

Bake in the centre of the oven for about 30 minutes or until golden brown and well risen, cooking a little longer if necessary. Best served while still warm.

HERMAN STARTER

HAWAII

When I was a child we used to make ginger beer and fed the starter two or three times a week, so I guess this recipe is not so very different but I had never heard of a Herman starter until I came across several recipes for Hawaiian Herman Cake. But I have since realised that there are many Hawaiian recipes which incorporate this starter and as is the way of things once I knew about it, I came across it many times.

1 envelope of dried yeast	150g/5oz plain flour
55ml/2fl oz water	300ml/1/2 pint milk
75g/3oz sugar	

Stir together the yeast and water in a small bowl, adding 1 tablespoon of the sugar. Set aside until the yeast becomes active and a froth forms.

Meanwhile in a separate bowl (not metal) stir together the remaining sugar, flour and milk. Slowly stir in the yeast mix, using a wooden spoon (to avoid metal reaction). Cover with a light cloth, cheesecloth is perfect, and leave in a warm place. Stir each day and add the feed detailed below, once a week.

50g/2oz sugar
150ml/1/4 pint milk
60g/21/2 oz flour

Use the starter as required. The starter may be stored in a refrigerator but will be slower to 'work'.

MARDI GRAS KING CAKE

USA

Twelve days after Christmas is traditionally the start of Mardi Gras, with its balls, parties and carnivals. In New Orleans the celebrations would not be complete without King Cakes, which are baked specially as part of the festivities. The King Cake's place in the day's celebrations is not unlike the English Twelfth Night Cake, which also has a hidden charm or bean in its midst, or the French Petit Noel or Little Christmas Cake. But the true feature of the Mardi Gras cake is without doubt the purple, green and gold coloured sugar crystals which are sprinkled over the top.

Although fairly easy to prepare and bake, the cakes are time consuming and each recipe that I have researched is a little different, some even have an elaborate filling of fruit and nuts. Essentially it is a rich brioche dough, enhanced by nutmeg, cinnamon and lemon or orange zest, and shaped into rings with a coin, china doll or bean hidden in the dough before baking; the finder of which becomes the Mardi Gras King or Queen for the day.

7g/¹/₂oz sachet of dried yeast	**Glaze**
2 tablespoons caster sugar	2 teaspoons rum
55ml/2fl oz lukewarm milk	175g/6oz icing sugar
	3 tablespoons hot water
375g/12oz plain flour	
1 teaspoon ground cinnamon	Coloured sugars, purple, green and gold
1 teaspoon ground nutmeg	
5 egg yolks	
Zest of a lemon	
175g/6oz cold butter	

In a small bowl, stir together the yeast, sugar and milk. Set aside in a warm place.

Measure the flour, cinnamon and nutmeg into a large bowl and after ten minutes stir in the yeast, which will by now be frothy. Using a pallet knife, stir while adding the egg yolks and lemon zest. Gather the mixture into a ball and transfer it onto a lightly floured surface. Knead by hand for about 10 minutes until the dough is smooth and springy.

Cut the cold butter into small pieces and knead them into the dough, a little at a time until it is fully incorporated. Lift the dough into a clean, lightly greased bowl, cover with a damp cloth and set aside in a warm place to double in size, which will take about an hour.

When risen, lift out the dough onto a lightly floured surface and knead for a few minutes before rolling the dough into a sausage shape.

Lift the cake onto a well-greased baking tray and pull the ends together, damping and sealing to form a ring. Push the china doll, coin (if using a coin wrap it carefully in foil) or bean into the cake before leaving the ring of cake in a warm place to double in size, about an hour. Preheat the oven to 180°C/350°F/Gas Mark 4.

BEIGNETS / FRITTERS

USA

Makes about 9 cakes

Originally a French recipe, Beignets have become a traditional sweet treat to be eaten with a coffee, particularly in the French Quarter of New Orleans where pavement cafés can be traced way back in the city's history.

4g/¹/₄oz dried yeast	1 large egg
120ml/4fl oz tepid water	100g/4oz caster sugar
2 teaspoons caster sugar	450g/1lb plain flour
	¹/₂ teaspoon ground cinnamon
175ml/6fl oz milk	¹/₂ teaspoon ground nutmeg
¹/₂ teaspoon vanilla extract	
50ml/2fl oz butter, melted	Caster sugar for sprinkling

In a small bowl stir together the yeast, tepid water and sugar, cover and leave in a warm place for 10 minutes.

Meanwhile in a large bowl mix together the milk, vanilla, butter, egg and sugar before stirring in the yeast. Stir in the flour and spices a little at a time, and then using your hands pull the mixture into a ball and transfer onto a lightly floured surface. Knead for about 10 minutes until the dough becomes smooth and elastic. Lift the ball of dough into a clean oiled bowl and cover with a tea cloth, transferring it to a warm place for the dough to double in size, which will take about an hour.

Turn the risen dough out onto a lightly floured surface and knead for a couple of minutes before rolling the dough into a sheet about 1cm/ ¹/₂in thick. Cut the dough into strips about 6cm/3in wide, cutting each strip at an angle, to form diamond shapes. Once all the dough has been used, cover the pieces with a cloth and leave the beignets to double in size, about 1 hour.

Heat an electric deep fryer to 180°C/350°F, dropping in a small piece of dough to check the temperature. The dough will rise quickly to the surface, bubbling if the oil is hot enough.

Fry the beignets 3 or 4 at a time, turning them over, as they become golden brown. About 5 minutes cooking time should be plenty for each batch.

Remove the cakes from the oil, and allow them to drain on a sheet of kitchen paper. Cover them with another sheet of paper and working quickly, complete the frying before lightly dusting the beignets with caster sugar. Serve with freshly ground coffee.

YEAST CAKES 79

KULICH

RUSSIA

Kulich is a Russian yeast cake served at Easter. It is traditionally baked in a special mould but you can use a clean baked bean tin to give the tall round shape. When the cake is cold it stands upright on a plate, is drizzled with white icing and topped with a flower or candle. The ingredients can vary; the spices used can be cinnamon, cardamom or saffron, with fruits ranging from just raisins to a wide range of dried fruits and peel. When slicing into rounds the Kulich may be served spread with jam or honey.

450g/1lb strong plain flour
1/2 teaspoon cardamom
1/2 teaspoon nutmeg
75g/3oz caster sugar
50g/2oz golden sultanas
50g/2oz currants
50g/2oz mixed peel
50g/2oz chopped blanched almonds

7g/1/4oz sachet easy blend yeast
300ml/1/2 pint milk
50g/2oz butter
1 beaten egg, save a spoonful for glazing

Icing
75g/3oz icing sugar
2 teaspoons lemon juice

Sift the flour and spices into a mixing bowl. Stir in the sugar, dried fruit, peel and chopped almonds before finally adding the dried yeast. Set the mixture aside. Gently warm the milk and butter in a small saucepan, stirring until dissolved. Allow to cool to blood temperature before beating in the egg. Make a well in the centre of the flour and fruit and pour in the milk, mixing until a soft dough is formed. Turn onto a lightly floured surface, knead until smooth; about 7-8 minutes. Put the dough into a clean bowl and cover with a damp tea towel before leaving in a warm place for about an hour or until doubled in size.

Grease and line the two suitable tins. Knead the dough for a couple of minutes, divide into two and shape into rounds before placing one into each mould. Set aside in a warm place and allow the dough to rise almost to the top. Preheat the oven to 190°C/375°F/Gas Mark 5.

Lightly brush the tops of the cakes with the remaining spoonful of beaten egg before baking for about 30 minutes or until a skewer inserted comes out cleanly. Cover with brown paper if the top browns too quickly. Leave for a few minutes before turning out onto a rack.

Sift the icing sugar into a small bowl and add enough lemon juice to form a thick icing. When the cakes are cold drizzle icing over the top (allowing it to run down the sides a little). Allow the icing to set before cutting into rounds. The Kulitch cakes are best eaten on the day of baking, but if this is not possible they may be frozen before icing.

When the dough has risen place the cake on the bottom rung of the oven and bake for about 30 minutes or until golden brown. Remove from the oven and slide onto a cooling rack, leaving the cake to become cold.

Stir the glaze ingredients together and brush over the top of the cake, sprinkling the coloured sugars onto the cake in the distinctive blocks of colour, green, purple and gold.

Place the decorated cake onto a serving plate together with decorations of your choice.

JULEKAGE / CHRISTMAS LOAF

NORWAY

Christmas would not be complete in Norway without this traditional yeasted Christmas loaf as a centrepiece. It is heavily fruited and lightly spiced and very similar versions are also baked in Denmark.

7g/¹/2oz packet active dry yeast
2 tablespoons warm water
300ml/¹/2 pint lukewarm milk
50g/2oz sugar
115g/4oz butter, melted
¹/2 teaspoon salt
1 teaspoon ground mace
1 egg, lightly beaten
450g/1lb plain flour

50g/2oz flaked almonds
115g/4oz golden raisins
115g/4oz chopped mixed peel

Icing/Decoration
115g/4oz icing sugar
2 tablespoons double cream
¹/4 teaspoon almond extract
Flaked almonds to sprinkle

In a medium bowl mix the yeast with the warm water and set aside to froth. After 10 minutes stir in the milk, sugar, melted butter, salt, mace and egg, beating gently until fully mixed together. Sift the flour into a large bowl and make a well in the centre. Pour the yeast mixture into the flour beating well. The resulting dough will be quite soft.

Set the bowl of dough aside, covering with a clean cloth and leave it to rise for about 30 minutes.

Remove the dough from its bowl and transfer to a lightly floured surface, kneading for about 10 minutes until smooth. Add the almonds, raisins and peel and knead until well mixed.

Place the dough back into a clean greased bowl, cover and leave to double in size, about 30-45 minutes.

Finally, knead gently and shape into a round cake, lift it into a 20cm/8in well butteredround cake tin, cover with a cloth and leave to double in size. Preheat the oven to 190°C/375°F/Gas Mark 5.

Bake the cake in the centre of the oven for about 25 minutes or until golden brown, when baked the cake should sound hollow when tapped. Turn the Julekage out onto a wire rack and leave to become completely cold.

In a small bowl, mix together the icing sugar, cream and almond extract, drizzling it over the top of the cake. Sprinkle the icing with a few flaked almonds, if liked.

KUGELHOPF

FRANCE

What an identity problem the Kugelhopf has; traditionally baked in the Alsace region of France, both Austria and Germany have also laid claim to the origins of this cake-bread.

Quite easy to prepare there are several variations, although the one given here is the most commonly eaten. It is always baked in a special round fluted cake tin with a hole in the centre.

15g/4oz mixed dried fruit	Zest of a lemon
2 tablespoons brandy	Zest of an orange
115g/4oz butter	450g/1lb bread flour
115g/4oz soft pale brown sugar	1 tablespoon dried yeast
3 eggs, lightly beaten	150ml/1/4 pint lukewarm milk

Mix the dried fruit and brandy together in a small bowl. Set aside.

Using an electric hand mixer, cream the butter and sugar until pale and fluffy. On a slow speed, mix in the eggs and the lemon and orange zest.

In a separate bowl, sift the flour and stir in the dried yeast.

Pour the butter, sugar and egg mixture into the flour, together with the lukewarm milk. Stir until the mixture comes together, cover the bowl with a clean cloth and leave to double in size, about 1 hour.

Finally stir in the fruit and brandy and spoon the mixture into a greased and floured Kugelhopf tin, smoothing the top. Cover and set aside to double in size, about an hour. Preheat the oven to 180°C/350°F/Gas Mark 4.

Cook in the centre of the oven for about 40 minutes or until golden brown. Leave to cool in the tin for about 10 minutes before turning out onto a wire cooling rack.

LARDY CAKE

WILTSHIRE, ENGLAND

Lardy cake most probably comes originally from Wiltshire, in the south west of England. There are many variations but the counties all have their own recipes adding various fruits and spices. There are also similar recipes from other regions such as Oxfordshire, Kent and Gloucestershire, Fourses cake in Sussex, Lardy Johns in Sussex but the Lardy cake seems to be the most well known. It is a very ancient recipe, probably medieval. Today it might be frowned upon as incredibly unhealthy, especially as the fat used is pork lard. However it is just not possible to substitute the pork lard for butter as it won't taste or look like a true lardy cake. It is usually baked as a square cake, but sometimes as buns.

450g/1lb yeast bread dough (page 19)	25 g/1oz mixed peel
150g /5oz pork lard	1/2 teaspoon mixed spice
150g/5oz pale brown sugar	1/2 teaspoon salt
50g/2oz currants	

Allow the dough to rise once and then roll into an oblong on a well-floured board. Dot two-thirds with half the lard and sprinkle with half the fruit. Fold into three, bringing the plain third over to the centre first and the remaining third over the top, pressing the edges together with a rolling pin. Give the dough a half turn and roll into an oblong again, repeating the process. Leave for 30 minutes in a warm place. Preheat the oven to 200°C/400°F/ Gas Mark 6.

Carefully lift the folded dough onto a large greased baking sheet and bake in the oven for about 35 minutes or until golden brown.

Remove from the baking sheet immediately and place on a plate. Serve hot spread with butter.

SPONGE AND MADEIRA CAKES

Though sponge cake is mentioned in a cookery book of 1615, it was not until much later, in the 18th century, that whisking eggs became an increasingly popular method of adding air into a cake mixture, giving a light, well-risen result. Whisking by hand can take a considerable amount of time so we are fortunate to have electric mixers today with much less arm ache involved.

A true sponge cake is made only from eggs, sugar and flour, no fat is included; the eggs and sugar being well whisked, before the flour is gently folded in. However the fat based Victoria Sandwich recipe, which was named for Queen Victoria in whose reign the cake was devised, has become popular. It is slightly more dense in texture but has the advantage of excellent keeping qualities.

It is interesting to see how various countries have adapted sponge cakes into very individual styles such as Sicilian Cassata, a truly delicious example, filled with luscious ingredients including ricotta cheese. One of the most widely eaten sponge cakes, the Swiss Roll, is wonderfully light and not as difficult to bake as it may at first seem.

I hesitated about including the Brazilian Bolo Bêbado cake but because it is prepared from breadcrumbs and flour there is no doubt that it has a sponge-like texture, helped by steeping it in rum syrup.

The Philippino Babingka also came into a very similar category, but I felt that the ingredients which include rice flour and coconut milk, do produce a sponge-like cake though it is perhaps nearer to a Madeira cake in texture. Madeira cake is a very distinctive, buttery but plain cake, with a little added lemon juice and a topping of citrus peel. The cake got its name from the glass of Madeira wine, with which it was traditionally served.

BRISTOL MADEIRA CAKE

ENGLAND

Perfect for afternoon tea on warm summer days, Madeira is a simple light textured cake, enhanced by the addition of a little grated lemon peel.

Originally devised in the 19th century as an accompaniment to the fortified sweet white wine from which it takes its name, it is believed to have originated in Bristol, an important centre for wine such as Bristol Cream and Bristol Milk which carry the city's name.

175g/6oz butter
175g/6oz caster sugar
285g/10oz self-raising flour
4 large eggs, beaten
Finely grated rind of one small lemon

Topping
3 thin slices of lemon peel

Preheat the oven to 180°C/350°F/Gas Mark 4. Cream butter and sugar together in a bowl until fluffy. Add the flour and eggs gradually, beating well after each addition. Then fold in the grated lemon rind.

Spoon the mixture into a 18cm/7in round greased and lined cake tin and smooth the top. Place in the centre of the oven for 30 minutes. Gently remove from the oven and working quickly, lay the citrus slices on top of the cake (I find the easiest kitchen tool to use is a potato peeler, which gives nice thin slices of the lemon rind) and return the cake to the oven. Bake for a further 30 minutes, checking occasionally until the cake is golden brown, well risen and firm when gently pressed on the top.

Remove from the oven and leave to cool in the tin for 10 minutes before turning out gently to cool on a wire rack.

SANDKAKA/SAND CAKE

SWEDEN

Sandkaka, moist and aromatic with a generous measure of brandy, is very similar to the Danish Sandkage, but there is no rice flour added, giving the Swedish cake a softer texture.

As the name suggests it is covered with 'sand' which in reality is the butter and breadcrumbs used to coat the inside of the cake tin.

25g/1oz butter, softened	225g/8oz self-raising flour
2 tablespoons dried breadcrumbs	1 teaspoon baking powder
	4 eggs, lightly beaten
225g/8oz butter	2 tablespoons brandy
225g/8oz caster sugar	

Grease a 20cm/8in ring cake tin with the softened butter, add the breadcrumbs and rotate the tin to cover the entire surface. Set it aside while you prepare the cake.

Preheat the oven to 180°C/350°F/Gas Mark 4. Cream the butter and sugar together until pale and creamy. Sift the flour and baking powder together.

Gently fold the flour, eggs and brandy into the creamed cake mixture, ensuring it is fully incorporated.

Finally spoon the mix into the greased cake tin and bake in the centre of the oven for about 40 minutes or until the cake feels firm and a skewer inserted into it comes out cleanly.

Allow the cake to stand a little before turning it onto a rack to become cool.

VICTORIA SANDWICH

ENGLAND

Queen Victoria lent her name to this traditional cake, which she was said to have greatly enjoyed with afternoon tea. Often confused with a sponge cake, which does not contain fat, it is baked in two shallow tins, sandwiched together with jam and finished on top with a light dusting of caster sugar. It is also excellent with a little butter cream sandwiched in along with the jam filling.

Incidentally, you can make this cake by the all-in-one method, but if you have time it is worth making it in the traditional way, as you will have a closer, better texture – the all-in-one method often results in large air holes.

115g/4oz butter	Jam
115g/4oz caster sugar	A little extra caster sugar
2 large eggs, lightly beaten	
115g/4oz self-raising flour	

Preheat the oven to 180°C/350°F/Gas Mark 4. Cream the butter and sugar until pale, light and fluffy. Fold in the eggs and the flour a little at a time until completely incorporated.

Spoon the mixture evenly into two greased 18cm/7in sandwich tins, smoothing the tops gently. Place in the centre of the oven, until well risen and golden. The top when lightly pressed should spring back. This will take approximately 25-30 minutes.

Remove from the tins and turn onto a cooling rack immediately. When completely cold, sandwich together with jam and sprinkle the top lightly with the caster sugar.

BOTERKOEK / BUTTER CAKE

HOLLAND

Sometimes researching cakes becomes not only a cookery lesson but a fascinating history and geography lesson as well. Some of the first settlers to Pennsylvania in the USA were the Dutch and they took their recipes for butter cakes with them so you find these cropping up in American cookbooks too. Perhaps because Butter Cake is easily baked and easily eaten.

On a slightly lighter note, one charming piece of folklore says that placing a Dutch Buckwheat Cake on your forehead will cure a headache. I have yet to try that form of alternative therapy.

250g/9oz self-raising flour
125g/4 1/2oz caster sugar
225g/8oz cold butter

I egg, lightly beaten
Finely grated rind of a lemon

Preheat the oven to 180°C/350°F/Gas Mark 4.

Measure the flour and sugar into a mixing bowl.

Cut the butter into very small pieces and add to the flour and sugar before rubbing it in quickly and lightly, keeping everything as cool as possible.

Add the egg and lemon rind, stirring with a pallet knife to form a ball.

Lift into a greased and lined 20cm/8in round cake tin and press down gently.

Bake in the centre of the oven for about 30 minutes or until golden brown and firm to touch when pressed gently in the centre.

Allow to cool completely before turning out onto a plate.

BABKA

POLAND   *Serves approximately 8*

The word Babka means Grandma, thus symbolising a loving person who takes time and care preparing simple but traditional foods. Hence a Babka is an unpretentious, delicately flavoured cake which has great prominence on Polish festive tables and especially within the country's Jewish communities. These old recipes passed down through families, also reflect a generation's change in lifestyle and in the case of a Babka, it can be made with yeast or as in the recipe here with self-raising flour, giving a more cake-like texture.

225g/8oz unsalted butter   275g/10oz self-raising flour
275g/10oz caster sugar   2 dessertspoons single cream
4 eggs, lightly beaten   3 teaspoons cocoa

Preheat the oven to 140°C/275°F/Gas Mark 1. Cream the butter and sugar together until light and fluffy, before slowly incorporating the eggs, flour and cream. Grease and line a 18cm/7in cake tin. Spoon one-third of the mixture into the cake tin and smooth.

Divide the remaining cake mix in half, and gently stir the cocoa into one of the portions. Spoon the chocolate mixture into the tin and lightly smooth, repeating with the remaining mix.

Place in the oven and bake for about one hour, or until well risen. The cake should feel firm when pressed lightly in the middle.

Allow to become cold before removing from the tin and placing onto a serving plate.

VINARTERTA HNODUD /
VIENNESE CAKE

ICELAND

To date, the only connection I have had with Iceland was through an amusing incident with my brother Andrew who, on a flight to Reykjavik found himself upgraded to first class and sitting next to an incredibly beautiful young woman. He chatted away feeling he was in with a chance but on landing she was swiftly ushered away and an air hostess asked him if he knew who he had been talking to – it was Miss Iceland who had been crowned Miss World a few days before.

Miss Iceland may not be remembered now but Vinarterta Hnodud certainly is. One of the most famous Icelandic cakes, it is said to have originated in Denmark, though quite why it is named Viennese Cake is unclear. However, its popularity and place as the celebration cake of Iceland is without question.

500g/1lb 2oz self-raising flour	900g/2lb pitted prunes
250g/9oz unsalted butter	Sugar to taste
250g/9oz caster sugar	1 knob of butter
2 eggs, lightly beaten	
	Topping
Filling	600ml/1 pint double cream
Rhubarb Jam or Prune Jam (recipe below)	Icing sugar

To make the filling cook the prunes in a little water until softened, before puréeing. When puréed add sugar to taste and a generous knob of butter, beating well together and allowing to cool before using.

Preheat the oven to 200°C/400°F/Gas Mark 6.

Place flour, softened butter and sugar into a large bowl and using your fingertips rub the mixture to form breadcrumbs. Add the lightly beaten eggs and using your hands firmly mix together until you have a ball of dough. Divide the dough into four. Place sheets of greaseproof paper onto two baking trays and roll the dough into rounds approximately 18cm/7in in diameter. Mark each round lightly with a fork and bake in the oven until pale golden brown and crisp. When baked, place on cooling racks to assemble when cold.

Spread a generous helping of jam onto three of the rounds and place them carefully on top of each other, finishing with the remaining cake. Finally, whisk the double cream, adding the icing sugar and when stiff spread over the top and sides of the cake. Serve immediately.

SANDKAGE / SAND CAKE

DENMARK

No Danish home would be complete without setting time aside for coffee and cake, while mulling over the events of the day. The breadcrumbs used to line the cake tin and the rice flour incorporated into the cake mixture, give added interest by their crunchy texture.

25g/1oz butter, softened
2 tablespoons dry breadcrumbs

Cake
225g/8oz butter
225g/8oz caster sugar

4 eggs, lightly beaten
150g/6oz self-raising flour
50g/2oz ground rice
Grated zest of lemon
1 tablespoon brandy, optional

Preheat the oven to 180°C/350°F/Gas Mark 4.

Spread the butter evenly around the base, middle and sides of the cake tin, before sprinkling the breadcrumbs around to coat the entire inside of the tin.

Using an electric hand mixer at high speed, cream the butter and caster sugar until pale and fluffy, before at the lowest speed, adding the eggs, flour, ground rice, lemon zest and brandy (if using) a little at a time until fully incorporated.

Finally, spoon the cake mixture evenly into a 20cm/8in round ring cake tin, gently smoothing the top.

Place into the oven and check after 45 minutes, when lightly pressed the top should feel springy. If not, return to the oven and check after a further 10 minutes until the cake is cooked.

Remove from the oven and immediately place a cake rack over the top and inverting it carefully, shake gently until you feel the cake drop from the tin.

Leave to become cold before transferring to a plate and serving.

TOSCATARTE

NORWAY

This incredibly rich cake, topped with a marvellous mix of caramel and almonds, while considered as Norwegian in origin, is actually very popular throughout Scandinavia.

2 large eggs	**Topping**
175g/6oz caster sugar	115g/4oz butter
50g/2oz melted butter	115g/4oz caster sugar
1 teaspoon vanilla extract	115g/4oz whipping cream
115g/4oz plain flour	115g/4oz flaked or slivered almonds
1 teaspoon baking powder	
3 tablespoons milk	

Preheat the oven to 180°C/350°F/Gas Mark 4.

Using a hand held mixer beat the eggs and sugar until thick, pale and creamy.

Using a large metal spoon, rotated in a figure of eight, add the remaining ingredients a little at a time. When fully mixed together, spoon the batter into a well greased 20cm/8in round loose bottomed cake tin and place in the centre of the oven. After about 25 minutes the cake will be golden brown and when the top is pressed gently, it will feel springy.

While the cake is cooking prepare the caramel topping. Melt the butter in a saucepan and add the sugar and cream, stirring constantly. Bring to the boil and cook for 2 to 3 minutes still stirring.

When the cake is taken from the oven, immediately pour over the caramel and sprinkle with the almonds. Place under a medium grill and cook until the topping is golden brown and bubbling, do not let it burn.

Allow to cool before removing from the tin; you will understand why a loose bottomed tin was so important. Eat while still warm – although it is still very good when cold.

CASSATA SICILIANA

SICILY

Cassata Siciliana is without doubt one of the most celebrated cakes to be made on the island of Sicily. Marsala, a sweet and aromatic Sicilian wine, is sprinkled liberally over each of the sponge layers before they are sandwiched together with the filling of ricotta cheese and chopped glacé fruits. The final decoration is a layer of almond paste over the cake, which may be topped with glacé fruits.

Several variations of Cassata cake can be found, usually named after the region in which they are baked. The oldest appears to be Cassata Palermitana, baked by the Italian, Francesco Leonardi (1750-1790) chef to Louis XV and Catherine II, who was perhaps more famous for making and writing books about soup. The finishing touches of the Palermitana are glacé icing before decorating with pistachio nuts and glacé fruits.

Sponge Base
175g/6oz butter
175g/6oz caster sugar
175g/6oz self-raising flour
3 large eggs, lightly beaten

3 tablespoons Marsala

Filling
350g/12oz ricotta cheese

115g/4oz mixed candied peel
115g/4oz plain chocolate chips
Juice of 1/2 lemon
Juice of 1/2 orange

Topping
450g/1lb almond paste
3 tablespoons sieved apricot jam
Glacé fruits to decorate

Preheat the oven to 180°C/350°F/Gas Mark 4. Cream the butter and sugar with an electric hand mixer until light and fluffy. Add the flour and the eggs a little at a time and mix until completely incorporated.

Spoon the mixture into a 20cm/8in round cake tin greased and lightly floured, and bake in the centre of the oven for 30-40 minutes or until firm to touch. Allow the cake to cool for 10 minutes before gently turning onto a wire rack.

When cold, slice the sponge into three horizontally and place one into the bottom of a 20cm/8in round cake tin lined with film before sprinkling with a tablespoonful of the Marsala. Combine the filling ingredients and smooth half of the mixture onto the sponge base smoothing before placing another sponge circle on the top of the filling. Repeat the same procedure again finally placing a weight on top of the third slice of sponge and place the cake in the refrigerator.

Roll the almond paste into a 20cm/8in circle large enough to cover the cake. Brush the cake with warmed apricot jam before carefully lifting the almond paste over the cake. Lift the cake carefully onto a plate and decorate with your favourite glacé fruits.

POPPY SEED SPONGE CAKE

POLAND

It is impossible to write about Poppy Seed Cake without pointing out the affection with which they are held in Poland, or indeed wherever Polish communities may have settled. It has remained of importance to Jews all over the world, in particular those whose families originated from Poland.

There are many different recipes – a sweet bread cake, rolled up with a layer of poppy seeds and raisins (see page 72), or this more straightforward, sponge cake mixture, into which poppy seeds and lemon juice have been added. I have included both recipes, simply because they are the most often used.

225g/8oz softened butter	100g/4oz poppy seeds
225g/8oz pale soft brown sugar	
4 eggs, lightly beaten	Zest and juice of 2 fresh lemons
225g/8oz self-raising flour	50g/2oz caster sugar

Preheat the oven to 180°C/350°F/Gas Mark 4.

Using a hand mixer, cream the butter and sugar together until pale and creamy. Continue beating very slowly while adding the eggs a little at a time, alternating with a tablespoonful of flour to ensure that the mixture does not curdle (the cake would taste just as good, but the texture would be spoilt).

Finally add the poppy seeds, stirring well and spoon the cake mixture into a greased and lined 20cm/8in cake tin. Cook in the centre of the oven for about 1 hour or until the cake is firm to touch and a skewer inserted into the centre, comes out cleanly.

While the cake is cooking measure the lemon juice and zest into a small saucepan together with the sugar and bring to a gentle rolling boil. Stir constantly and when the sugar has dissolved simmer for a further 3 or 4 minutes before removing from the heat and allowing to cool.

When the cake is cooked, leave it in its tin for a few minutes before gently turning it out onto a cooling rack and pour the lemon syrup over the cake, being careful to ensure that the cake absorbs all the liquid. You might find it helpful to pierce the top of the cake in several places.

This cake should be kept in an airtight container and eaten within a couple of days.

CASSAVA CAKE

BRAZIL

The tuberous roots of the sweet cassava plant, widely grown in Brazil, have many uses. Their starch content forms the basis for tapioca pudding and by contrast laundry starch. Cassava, also known as Yucca, can sometimes be found in good specialist food shops.

Traditionally served with strong dark Brazilian coffee for breakfast, Cassava cake is very moist and will sink when taken from the oven, so don't be alarmed; this is just as it should be.

450g/1lb cassava root
150g/5oz butter
450g/1lb caster sugar

1 egg, lightly beaten
175ml/6fl oz thick coconut milk

Preheat the oven to 190°C/375°F/Gas Mark 5.

Peel the cassava, grate finely and set aside.

In a separate bowl beat together the butter and sugar, using a hand held electric mixer. Cream until light and fluffy, slowly add the egg and coconut milk stirring constantly. Finally stir in the grated cassava root.

Grease and lightly flour a 20cm/8in square cake tin. Pour the mixture evenly into the tin, lightly smoothing the surface with the back of a spoon. Bake for about 30-40 minutes or until a skewer inserted into the centre comes out cleanly.

Cool in the tin before cutting the cake into squares.

BIBINGKA / RICE CAKES

PHILIPPINES

Probably the most widely eaten cake in the Philippine Islands, Babingka are sweet rice cakes which are often eaten for breakfast and can always be readily found on roadside food stalls.

At Christmas Babingka really come into their own, when they are traditionally eaten as one of the festive foods. I came across many differing recipes for the little cakes, but settled on the one which appeared to be the most widely baked.

350g/12oz soft pale brown sugar
115g/4oz butter, melted
5 eggs, lightly beaten
600ml/1 pint coconut milk
450g/1lb rice flour
2 tablespoons baking powder

Topping
Desiccated coconut (optional)

Preheat the oven to 180°C/350°F/Gas Mark 4.

Mix together the sugar and butter in a large bowl. Using an electric hand mixer, slowly add the eggs and coconut milk.

Sift the rice flour and baking powder together and mix into the batter, blending the mixture until it is lump free.

Pour into a well greased, shallow 23x30cm/9x12in cake tin and bake for about 35 minutes or until the cake is golden brown and feels just firm to touch.

Remove from the oven and allow the cake to cool before cutting into portions. If liked, the cake can be sprinkled with desiccated coconut to serve.

1 2 3 4 CAKE

USA

Though the 1 2 3 4 Cake is generally seen as an American cake it does share a lot in common with other cakes baked throughout the world before the days of formal measurements and recipes when the unit of measure was the cup. The original 1 2 3 4 Cake recipe was recorded in the simplest form enabling it to be passed between family and friends. Today the standard US cup measures 225ml/8fl oz.

1 cup of butter	3 cups of flour
2 cups of sugar	4 eggs

Preheat the oven to 160°C/325°F/Gas Mark 3. Cream the butter and sugar together until pale and fluffy. Beat the flour and eggs into the mixture, a little at a time. Spoon the cake mixture into a greased and lightly floured 18cm/7in cake tin and gently smooth the top.

Place the cake in the centre of the oven and cook for about 45 minutes or until golden brown and it feels firm when pressed gently in the middle. All ovens vary and if the cake needs to cook a little longer this is quite acceptable.

When baked, turn the cake out onto a wire cooling rack and leave to become cold before lifting onto a serving plate and sprinkling with a little caster sugar.

ANGEL CAKE

USA

Seen as typically American, Angel Cake is baked in a ring mould and is just heavenly when served with fresh raspberries or strawberries. What makes it so special is that it contains neither butter nor egg yolks, giving it its characteristic white appearance and very light texture. Angel Cakes look extremely pretty if, when completely cold, they are lightly sprinkled with sifted icing sugar and finished with a fresh flower – a rose is just perfect.

150g/5oz plain flour	1/2 teaspoon almond extract
300g/10oz caster sugar	2 teaspoons lemon juice
10 egg whites	
1 teaspoon cream of tartar	A little sifted icing sugar
1 teaspoon vanilla extract	

Preheat the oven to 180°C/350°F/Gas Mark 4. Sift together the flour and half the caster sugar. Repeat the sifting three times. I find it best to sift onto a sheet of greaseproof paper.

In a large bowl, whisk the egg whites until they form soft peaks. Add the cream of tartar and the remaining sugar a little at a time, continuing to whisk until they form fairly stiff peaks again. Stir in the vanilla and almond extract together with the lemon juice.

Using a metal spoon gently fold in the sifted flour and sugar using a figure of eight movement to ensure you do not lose all the air you have just worked so hard to put in. Finally spoon the cake mix into a lightly greased and floured 25cm/10in Angel cake tin. Smooth gently and put into the oven, to bake for about 50 minutes. When cooked the top of the cake will be pale golden brown and when lightly pressed will feel springy.

When cooked leave the cake in the tin and place a cooling rack over the top, gently turn the cake upside down and leave to become completely cold on the rack, cake tin still in place.

When cold, remove the tin, place the cake onto a plate and sift a little icing sugar over the top.

BOLO BÊBADO / DRUNKEN CAKE

BRAZIL

This very popular rum sponge cake can be served with fruit or sprinkled with icing sugar. Made with flour and dry breadcrumbs, the texture is a little different to a European sponge cake, but steeped in rum syrup the Bolo Bêbado is not only aromatic but absolutely delicious.

350g/12oz caster sugar	**Rum Syrup**
225g/8oz dry breadcrumbs	115g/4oz granulated sugar
115g/4oz plain flour	150ml/5fl oz water
1 tablespoon baking powder	150ml/5fl oz white rum
6 large eggs	
	Icing sugar, for decoration

Preheat the oven to 180°C/350°F/Gas Mark 4.

Measure all the cake ingredients into a food processor and mix on a high speed until the ingredients are thoroughly blended and smooth.

Pour the mixture into a buttered and lined 20cm/8in square cake tin and bake in the centre of the oven for about 20-25 minutes or until a skewer inserted into the middle of the cake, comes out cleanly. When baked, leave the cake to cool in its tin for about 20 minutes, while you prepare the syrup.

Measure the syrup ingredients into a small saucepan. Stirring constantly bring to the boil before turning down the heat and allowing the syrup to simmer for 10 minutes.

Turn the cake out onto a serving plate, remove the greaseproof paper and slowly pour the rum syrup evenly over the top.

Allow the cake to become almost completely cold before lightly sprinkling with sifted icing sugar. Best eaten on the day of baking but still pretty good the next day.

BUCHE DE NOËL

CANADA

Gathering together around a log fire is so much part of winter festivities so it is no surprise to find that both in France and Quebec, the French have been devoted to a log shaped cake, the Buche de Noël. Traditionally served on Christmas Day, this chocolate roulade has chestnut purée and fresh cream blended together to fill and ice this delectable cake. It can then be decorated with a sprig of fresh holly and sprinkled with icing sugar 'snow'.

Sponge base	Chestnut and cream filling
6 large eggs, separated	275ml/10fl oz double cream
150g/5oz caster sugar	175g/6oz sweetened chestnut purée
50g/2oz cocoa	(available tinned)
25g/1oz self-raising flour	1 tablespoon rum (optional)

Preheat the oven to 180°C/350°F/Gas Mark 4 and line a Swiss roll tin 33x23cm/13x9in, with non-stick paper.

Put the yolks into a bowl with the caster sugar and using a hand held electric whisk, whisk until they become pale and increase in volume, so that a little trailed over the mixture should keep its shape. In a separate bowl whisk the egg whites until stiff.

Sift the cocoa and flour onto a sheet of greaseproof paper and tip it gently into the egg yolk mixture and using a figure of eight action fold it in with a metal spoon. Add the egg whites very gently, using the same figure of eight, so that you do not lose the air you have so carefully whisked in. Pour the sponge evenly into the lined tin, ensuring the mixture goes right into the corners and bake it for about 20 minutes in the centre of the oven until well risen and springy to touch. Lightly sprinkle icing sugar onto a sheet of greaseproof paper larger than the tin size, ready for when you bring the cake out of the oven.

Gently turn the roulade upside down onto the prepared greaseproof paper and carefully peel the baking paper away. Finally, using the baking paper to help you roll up the roulade gently and after covering it with a tea towel, leave to become cold. Incidentally if the cake cracks a little, it really does not matter, it will add to its charm.

Whip the double cream until it stands in soft peaks. Measure the chestnut purée into a bowl and stir in the rum and a little cream to soften it, before folding in the remaining whipped cream. Gently unroll the roulade and spread with half the filling, gently rolling it back up before cutting a 5cm/2in section and attaching it to the side of the cake to act as a branch.

Finally, spread the remaining chestnut and cream mixture over the top of the cake making a pattern to resemble bark, this is easiest if you use a fork. Decorate as liked.

BANANA CAKE

USA

Always popular in America and certainly now very popular here in England, a banana cake does not seem to have a real history other than that it is really great to eat and simple to make and probably came about as a way to use up overripe bananas.

225g/8oz plain flour	225g/8oz soft pale brown sugar
1 teaspoon baking powder	3 eggs, lightly beaten
1/2 teaspoon bicarbonate of soda	4 medium bananas, mashed
115g/4oz softened butter	50g/2oz chopped pecan nuts

Preheat the oven to 180°C/350°F/Gas Mark 4. Sift the flour, baking powder and bicarbonate of soda into a bowl.

In a separate bowl, using an electric mixer, cream the butter and sugar until light and fluffy.

On a low speed add the flour and eggs, a little at a time, to prevent curdling.

Finally stir in the mashed bananas and pecan nuts. Spoon the cake mixture into a greased and lightly floured 20cm/8in cake tin and cook for about 40 minutes or until the top feels springy, when pressed gently in the centre.

Remove the cake from the oven and turn out onto a wire cooling rack. Leave to become completely cold before serving.

PINEAPPLE UPSIDE-DOWN CAKE

USA

In the past white sugar was very expensive and so was rarely used; hence most cakes were baked with the much less costly brown sugar. This pineapple upside-down cake is particularly delicious when baked with dark brown sugar.

The bottom of the cake tin is spread with a layer of butter and sprinkled generously with dark brown sugar and pineapple slices are laid decoratively on top. A rich sponge cake mixture is spread evenly over the pineapple and when baked the cake is turned upside down onto a serving plate and eaten while still warm.

115g/4oz butter	175g/6oz butter
115g/4oz soft dark brown sugar	175g/6oz soft pale brown sugar
1 fresh pineapple cut into rings	175g/6oz self-raising flour
Glacé cherries	3 large eggs, lightly beaten

Preheat the oven to 180°C/350°F/Gas Mark 4. In a small saucepan melt the butter and soft dark brown sugar and spread the mixture over the bottom of a lightly greased 23cm/9in round cake tin.

Arrange the pineapple rings in a decorative pattern on the base of the cake tin, putting a glacé cherry in the centre of each pineapple ring. Set the cake tin aside while you prepare the sponge mixture.

Using an electric hand held mixer, cream the butter and sugar until pale and fluffy. Add the flour and lightly beaten eggs, a little at a time. Finally spoon the sponge mixture over the pineapple layer in the bottom of the cake tin. Smooth the top and place the cake into the centre of the ovenfor about 30 minutes or a little longer, until the sponge is just firm to touch.

When cooked remove from the oven and immediately turn it out onto a serving plate. Do be very careful though not to burn yourself when you turn out the cake as the butter and sugar syrup will be very hot.

Allow to cool before serving. Your decorative pineapple will now be on the top of your cake.

POUND CAKE

ENGLAND

While crediting the Pound Cake to England, it is only fair to say that very similar cake recipes can be found throughout the USA and parts of Europe. Rather like the 12 3 4 cake, the Pound Cake was quite simply a way of remembering the ingredients and their weight, despite little or no access to recorded recipes or the use of any advanced kitchen equipment.

It is a fairly dense cake but can be enlivened with alcohol steeped fruit such as cherries or sultanas.

1lb butter softened	8 eggs, lightly beaten
1lb caster sugar	2 teaspoons vanilla extract
1lb self-raising flour	

Preheat the oven to 190°C/375°F/Gas Mark 5. Using a hand held electric mixer, cream the butter and sugar together until pale and fluffy.

On a low speed, mix in a tablespoon of flour and a tablespoon of lightly beaten egg, repeating until all the ingredients are fully incorporated, finally adding the vanilla extract.

Spoon the mixture into two greased and floured 900g/2lb loaf tins and bake in the centre of the oven for about 45 minutes or until the tops feel firm and a skewer inserted in the cake comes out cleanly.

Allow the cakes to cool for about 10 minutes before turning out onto a wire cooling rack and leaving to become completely cold – although it is a very good cake to eat while slightly warm.

WHITE MOUNTAIN CAKE

USA

Sister Jennie's Shaker Desserts is the title of a little paperback published in Ohio 25 years ago, which details all the pudding and cake recipes she held precious. Sister Jennie was described as 'sprightly, with a no nonsense air about her' and one of the things she left as her legacy was a small leather-bound notebook containing Shaker recipes in her handwriting. Sadly Sister Jennie died in 1956 but her little book of recipes, described as 'like Sister Jennie and the Shakers, plain and wholesome, simple and good', will always be treasured. This White Mountain Cake stood out as my chosen recipe, perhaps because it dates back to the 1880s.

540g/1lb 2oz plain flour
350g/12oz caster sugar
3 teaspoons baking powder
125g/4oz butter, softened

2 eggs, not beaten
250ml/9fl oz milk
2 teaspoons vanilla extract

Preheat the oven to 180°C/350°F/Gas Mark 4. Sift the flour into a mixing bowl and add the sugar and baking powder. Stir together.

Add the softened butter and gently rub it in using your fingertips.

Add the eggs and stir until fully incorporated. Finally, add the milk and vanilla extract and stir thoroughly.

Spoon into a well greased and lightly floured 900g/2lb loaf tin. Bake for about 25-30 minutes in the centre of the oven until the cake is springy to the touch and a dry skewer inserted into the centre of the cake, comes out cleanly. Allow to cool a little before turning out onto a rack.

SWISS ROLL

ENGLAND

From the very name of this delicious cake, it is clear that it probably did not have its origins in this country. But given the length of time it has been served at our tea tables I've put it in as an English cake. It is certainly a little time consuming but a good homemade Swiss Roll bears no resemblance to one bought from a supermarket. And like any sponge cake, the finished result corresponds exactly to the care taken in preparation.

3 large eggs
85g/3½oz caster sugar
85g/3½oz plain flour
1 tablespoon hot water

Filling
Raspberry jam or lemon curd
A little extra caster sugar

Preheat the oven to 200°C/400°F/Gas Mark 6.

Half fill a saucepan with boiling water and place a large mixing bowl on the top. Break the eggs into the bowl and add the sugar, whisking constantly until the mixture is thick enough to leave a trail when the whisk is held above the bowl. By this time the egg mixture will be very pale and have increased in volume.

Remove the bowl from the heat. Sift the flour a little at a time, over the mixture and using a large metal spoon and a figure of eight motion, carefully fold in. Once the flour has been added, working quickly, add the hot water to slacken the mixture and immediately pour the mixture into a greased and lined Swiss Roll tin. Allow the mixture to run into the corners of the tin by tilting, but do not smooth the top. Once it uniformly covers the tin, bake immediately for 10 to 15 minutes, until well risen and firm to touch. Do not overcook!

Meanwhile dredge a sheet of greaseproof paper with caster sugar and immediately invert the cake onto the paper, remove the tin and allow to cool for 10 minutes, before gently removing the baking paper from the cake. Trim the edges of the cake slightly, to make it easier to roll.

Spread the Swiss Roll with the jam or lemon curd, smoothing it to the edges.

Lift the greaseproof paper from the short edge and roll. Don't worry if the surface cracks, it really doesn't matter, it all adds to the 'homemade' charm. Dredge lightly with caster sugar and place on a plate to serve.

PASTRY CAKES

This section contains a great variety of interesting and unusual cakes. There are Danish Pastries, made from a very rich buttery, flaky pastry. Croquembouche, Gateau Saint Honoré and éclairs are all baked from a basic choux pastry, albeit the Saint Honoré also involves puff pastry, but they could not be more different; éclairs are simple small cakes, which taste wonderful filled with fresh cream and drizzled with melted chocolate, while Saint Honore and Croquembouche are far more elaborate.

Greek Baklava, Moroccan Serpent Cakes and M'Hanncha are all made from filo pastry but it produces totally different results. The Greek Baklava cakes are baked as layers of nuts and filo steeped in a citrus and spice syrup while Moroccan Serpent Cake is literally baked in a snake shape, with layers of filo rolled around 'sausages' of almond filling. Filo pastry is not something I have ever tried to make as great skill and experience is required to roll the pastry thinly enough but in any event excellent ready prepared sheets can be bought from the chilled or freezer cabinets of your local delicatessen or supermarket. The important thing to remember is not to let the sheets dry out. Once they have been unrolled from their packaging, cover them with a damp cloth until they have been coated with melted butter, ready to use.

In total contrast to those Middle Eastern sweet confections the Scottish Black Bun Cake and the Chinese Moon Cakes are both literally cake 'pies'; with a traditional filling baked in a pastry case, albeit their fillings are totally different, both are part of a festive tradition. The Scottish Black Bun Cakes are cooked and served during the Christmas and New Year celebrations and the Moon Cakes are baked especially for the Chinese Autumn Moon Festival.

CROQUEMBOUCHE

FRANCE

A visually stunning cake, which often forms the centrepiece at a French wedding or christening, Croquembouche comes from the words *croquem* meaning crackles and *bouche* meaning mouth.

While not really difficult to prepare, it does require patience, an artistic eye and a steady hand. Little choux buns are built into a pyramid secured by a caramel sauce, which forms the 'glue'. Sometimes a special mould is used to build the pyramid but as they are not easily available you may prefer to pile the little buns freehand.

Choux pastry	**Filling**
225g/8oz unsalted butter	450ml/3/4 pint double cream
200ml/7fl oz water	2 tablespoons icing sugar
200ml/7fl oz milk	
1 dessertspoonful caster sugar	**Caramel sauce**
225g/8oz plain flour, sifted	175g/6oz granulated sugar
6 large eggs	250ml/9fl oz water

Preheat the oven to 200°C/400°F/Gas Mark 6. Place the butter, water, milk and sugar into a medium saucepan and bring to the boil stirring constantly. Remove from the heat and add the sifted flour, continuing to stir vigorously. Cook the flour paste for a couple of minutes over a low heat, continuing to stir constantly. Remove from the heat and beat in the eggs one at a time. The choux mixture is now ready to use. Spoon into a large piping bag with a plain nozzle and pipe the little round buns (about 2.5cm/1in in diameter) onto large greased baking sheets. Continue until all the mix has been used. Fifty little buns will pile into a cake about 22-25cm/9-10in high.

Place the trays into the oven and bake the buns for 10-15 minutes until well risen and golden brown. Do not over bake. Remove from the baking trays and transfer immediately onto a wire rack to cool.

Pour the double cream, together with the icing sugar into a bowl and whisk until stiff. Pipe a little filling into the centre of each choux bun.

For the sauce place the sugar and water into a small saucepan and bring rapidly to the boil, do not stir but swirl the pan frequently until the sugar melts. Boil on a high heat until the sugar becomes golden brown. This takes about 5 minutes.

Remove from the heat and immediately place the saucepan into cold water to stop the caramel from continuing to cook. Allow the caramel to cool before dipping each choux bun into the sauce and begin to build the pyramid by placing a circle of them on a serving plate, glueing them together with the caramel, decreasing each circle in size until finally finishing with one perfect choux bun on top. Finish the pyramid by drizzling with the remaining caramel and place single flowers of your choice onto the top and sides of the cake – six flower heads should be plenty. Best eaten on day of preparation.

GALETTE DES ROIS / THREE KINGS' CAKE

FRANCE

It is very hard to think of French cakes without lingering over the famous Marie Antoinette quote, *Qui'ils mangent de la brioche* – Let them eat cake. For indeed the French have a large diversity of cakes, many with pastry as a main ingredient and the Galette des Rois is a perfect example. Some areas do have slightly different versions of the recipe, but this is a particularly delectable almond recipe native to Paris.

This is one of the first French cakes I ever baked and is traditionally cooked to celebrate Epiphany. A bean or charm is baked in the filling and the recipient considered blessed with good luck.

125g/5oz unsalted butter	1 dessertspoonful Cointreau
125g/5oz soft pale brown sugar	3 eggs, lightly beaten
175g/6oz ground almonds	2 slices ready-bought puff pastry

Preheat the oven to 200°C/400°F/Gas Mark 6. Cream the butter and sugar until light and fluffy and gradually incorporate the ground almonds and Cointreau, together with enough beaten egg to form into a soft paste. Set the remaining egg aside.

Roll the puff pastry into two 25cm/10in circles and place one onto a well-greased baking tray.

Spread the almond mixture over the puff pastry, to within 3cm/1in of the edge. Brush the edge with beaten egg and place the second pastry circle over the top of the mixture, pressing the edges together carefully.

Finally, with a sharp knife, cut a little into the top forming a diamond pattern. Brush the top with the remaining egg and place into the oven and bake for 30 minutes until puffed and golden brown.

Delicious served warm but equally good eaten cold.

GATEAU SAINT HONORÉ

FRANCE

The story goes that during the 19th century a pâtissier Monsieur Chiboust had a baker's shop in the Rue Saint Honoré in Paris and created this elaborate cake to honour Saint Honoré, who was the Bishop of Amiens in the 6th century and became the patron saint of bakers and pastry chefs. Today it can be found around the world on almost every Christmas table in households wanting to preserve their French backgrounds. A perfect example of how traditional foods can travel from one side of the world to another.

Not an easy cake to make, allow plenty of time, but the end result is well worth the effort. However for the first stage there is absolutely no crime in using a pack of the excellent frozen or chilled puff pastry readily available in the shops, as it is simply impossible to make a good puff pastry without taking considerable time and trouble.

Puff pastry
450g/1lb plain flour
1/2 teaspoon salt

450g/1lb butter
100ml/4fl oz very cold water

Sift the flour and salt into a large bowl and add 50g/2oz of the slightly softened butter, rub into the flour until it resembles fine breadcrumbs. Add enough water to form a soft dough and turn the pastry out onto a lightly floured board, kneading gently until smooth.

Roll the pastry into an oblong and dot half the remaining butter onto one half. Fold the other half of the pastry over the buttered area and roll out the pastry again into an oblong, repeating the process with the remaining butter. Wrap the pastry in cling film and leave in a cool place such as the refrigerator for about 30 minutes to allow it to settle.

Next stage: Roll the dough into an oblong again, being careful not to let any of the butter break through the surface of the pastry and then fold it into three and return in cling film to the refrigerator for a further 45 minutes, it is this folding which gives the pastry its characteristic layers.

Repeat the process twice more and then the pastry is ready to use. You will be able to see the layers you have formed in the pastry dough, during all the folding and rolling. Allow to rest for 15 minutes before placing on a lightly floured surface and rolling into a 20cm/8in circle. Prick all over with a skewer before placing in a cool place while you make the choux dough.

Choux pastry
120g/4oz unsalted butter
150ml/1/4 pint water
150ml/1/4 pint milk

1 dessertspoonful caster sugar
120g/4oz plain flour, sifted
3 large eggs

Preheat the oven to 200°C/400°F/Gas Mark 6. Place the butter, water, milk and sugar into a medium saucepan and bring to the boil stirring constantly. Remove from the heat and add the sifted flour, continuing to stir vigorously. Cook the flour paste for a couple of minutes over a low heat, still continuing to stir. Remove from the heat and beat in the eggs a little at a time.

The choux mixture is now ready to use. Spoon half the mixture into a large piping bag with a plain 1cm/1/2in nozzle. Remove the puff pastry circle from the refrigerator, place on a non-stick baking tray and beginning on the outer edge, pipe a spiral of the mixture to cover the base. Finally using the remaining mixture pipe little buns, (about 2.5cm/1in diameter), onto a large lightly floured non-stick baking sheet. Continue until all the mix has been used.

Place both the trays into the oven and bake for 10-15 minutes until well risen and golden brown. Do not over bake. The small buns may be ready sooner in which case gently remove from the oven and allow the base to bake a little more until cooked. Remove from the baking trays and transfer immediately to wire racks to cool.

Crème pâtissière

3 egg yolks
150g/5oz caster sugar
40g/1 1/2oz plain flour

300ml/1/2 pint milk
150ml/1/4 pint double cream
1 tablespoon Cointreau (optional)

In a small bowl blend the egg yolks, sugar and flour into a smooth paste. In a medium saucepan bring the milk to the boil and then pour a little at a time onto the paste, stirring quickly before pouring back into the saucepan. On a low heat, stirring constantly allows it to cook gently until it thickens. Remove the pan from the heat and allow to cool before stirring in the lightly whipped double cream and the Cointreau, if using.

Using half of the crème pâtissière fill a piping bag and put a little crème into each of the choux buns. The remaining crème will be used to decorate the top of the cake.

Caramel

175g/6oz granulated sugar
250ml/9fl oz water

Place the sugar and water into a small saucepan and bring rapidly to the boil, do not stir but swirl the pan frequently until the sugar melts. Boil on a high heat until the sugar becomes golden brown. This takes about 5 minutes. Remove from the heat and immediately place the saucepan into cold water to stop the caramel from continuing to boil. Allow the caramel to cool before dipping each choux bun into the mixture and placing in a ring on the outer edge of the cake base.

Pipe the crème pâtissière into the centre of the cake and use any remaining choux buns to form an attractive pattern. Finally drizzle the remaining caramel onto the top of the cake adding a little fresh fruit such as raspberries if liked.

BLACK BUN

SCOTLAND

One of my most vivid and happy memories of living in Scotland was Hogmanay, 31st December, where First Footing is an essential part of the festive celebrations. A tall dark stranger bearing a lump of coal must be the first to set foot over the doorstep, in order to ensure good luck for the coming year and he in turn should be greeted with a dram of whisky and a slice of Black Bun. Formerly served on Twelfth Night, the cake became known as Scottish Christmas Bun although this was eventually shortened to Black Bun. It is a very rich dark fruit cake, encased in shortcrust pastry, it takes time and patience to make but is well worthwhile as it is really quite delicious. Baked several weeks in advance and stored until fully matured, it will keep well for up to four or five months.

350g/12oz shortcrust pastry	350g/12oz sultanas
	350g/12oz currants
Filling	115g/4oz chopped glacé peel
225g/8oz plain flour	115g/4oz pale muscovado sugar
1 teaspoon bicarbonate of soda	115g/4oz blanched chopped almonds
1 teaspoon mixed spice	5 tablespoons milk
1 teaspoon ground ginger	1 egg, lightly beaten
1 teaspoon ground cinnamon	2 tablespoons whisky
1 teaspoon ground mace	
1 teaspoon baking powder	**Glaze**
115g/4oz raisins	1 beaten egg

Roll two-thirds of the pastry into a large circle, use it to line the bottom and sides of a greased 20cm/8in loose bottomed round cake tin, carefully pressing it into the corners. Place the tin in the refrigerator together with the remaining third of the pastry, wrapped in cling film, ready to use for the lid, while you make the filling,

Preheat the oven to 180°C/350°F/Gas Mark 4. Sift the flour, bicarbonate of soda, spices and baking powder into a bowl and add the dried fruit, sugar and chopped nuts stirring thoroughly. Pour in the milk; add the lightly beaten egg and finally the whisky, then using a pallet knife stir the mixture until it forms a pliable dough.

Spoon the mixture into the lined pastry case, pressing carefully with your fingers, to ensure there are no gaps, finally smoothing the top. Roll the remaining pastry into a circle of approximately 23cm/9in, dampening the edges with water and place evenly over the fruit, sealing the edges together with finger and thumb, to produce a fluted edge. Glaze the top of the pastry cake with the beaten egg and make two or three holes in the surface, using a skewer. Bake in the oven for 2 1/2-3 hours, covering the top with brown paper if the cake begins to darken too quickly. Remove from the oven and leave the cake for at least 1 hour before removing carefully from the tin and lifting onto a wire rack to become completely cold. Finally wrap the cake in greaseproof and foil and store in a cool, dry place.

GUR CAKE

The background to this cake is rather intriguing. Dublin bakers are said to have devised the recipe to use up their day old bread and cakes, making it an economical and inexpensive tummy filler. Particularly popular with children playing truant from school, or as it was known 'on the gur', it sold at only half an old penny for a generous square.

Still baked by a few Dublin bakers, this recipe is for a rather more upmarket version, using plain cake rather than bread but of course, you may use breadcrumbs.

Short crust pastry
225g/8oz plain flour
115g/4oz butter
Cold water to mix

Filling
225g/8oz stale plain cake crumbs
3 tablespoons plain flour
1/2 teaspoon baking powder
2 teaspoons mixed spice

115g/4oz dried mixed fruit
25g/1oz mixed candied peel
50g/2oz pale soft brown sugar
50g/2oz butter, melted
1 egg, lightly beaten
A little milk to bind

Topping
One beaten egg
Caster sugar to sprinkle

To make the pastry measure the flour and butter into a bowl and using your fingertips rub it together until it looks like breadcrumbs. Add enough cold water to pull the mixture into a ball, bearing in mind that you should handle the dough gently. Grease a 20x30cm/8x12in square baking tin with butter. Divide the pastry in two and roll each piece out to measure the size and shape of the tin. Place one sheet of pastry in the bottom of the cake tin and put aside to prepare the filling. Preheat the oven to 190°C/375°F/Gas Mark 5.

Measure all the dry ingredients into a bowl and stir with a pallet knife until well mixed, add the melted butter, lightly beaten egg and a little milk to bind. Spoon the cake filling into the prepared tin, spreading it evenly over the pastry. Finish by placing the second sheet on top and brush with a little beaten egg.

Put the cake into the oven, where it will need only about 20 minutes to cook. Sprinkle it with a little caster sugar while still hot. Allow to cool in the tin before cutting into generous squares.

BAKLAVA

Makes 16

Baklava is traditionally served on festive days; utterly delectable sweet and aromatic little pastries, packed with chopped nuts such as almonds and bright green pistachios, are topped with highly scented syrup. Wonderful served with strong black coffee.

Thinking about these little cakes and my first experience of them, brings back memories of climbing down a rickety ladder over the side of a large ferry into a tiny boat and being rowed to the harbour side at Mykonos, long before it became a tourist destination. There was an abundance of strongly scented flowers competing with the intense aroma of roasting coffee beans, food cooking in the open air and honey so aromatic that I realised I had never really tasted honey before.

50g/2oz blanched almonds, chopped
50g/2oz pistachio nuts, chopped
50g/2oz soft pale brown sugar
150g/6oz unsalted butter, gently melted
6 sheets of filo pastry

Syrup
150g/6oz caster sugar
300ml/1/2 pint water
Juice and rind of 1/2 lemon
Juice and rind of 1/2 orange
1/2 whole cinnamon stick
2 green cardamom pods, crushed lightly

Preheat the oven to 180°C/350°F/Gas Mark 4. Grease a 18x28cm/7x11in shallow baking tin.

Mix together the almonds, pistachios and sugar. Trim the sheets of filo to fit exactly into the tin, placing one into the bottom of the tin. Brush with butter and sprinkle a little of the nut and sugar mixture evenly over the sheet. Repeat, brushing the filo pastry with liberal amounts of butter between each layer. Finish with a sheet of filo and again brush with the last of the melted butter.

Gently press around the edges with your hands, to seal the edges, before marking the top into diamonds, using a very sharp knife.

Place into the centre of the oven and bake until golden brown and puffy, about 25 minutes.

Meanwhile put the sugar, water, citrus juices, rind and spices in a small saucepan, and bring to the boil, bubbling gently for 5 minutes. Set aside to cool a little and then sieve to remove the spices and rind.

When cooked, remove the Baklava from the oven and place the tin on a wire rack. Working quickly, pour the syrup evenly over the cake. Set aside to cool overnight, allowing the flavours to intermingle. Before serving, cut the Baklava into the marked diamonds and serve in portions.

CRULLERS

One thing which has become very apparent while researching international cakes, is the way in which the same cake appears in neighbouring countries, albeit often under a different or somewhat similar name. Crullers are a good example, traditionally baked in Iceland, these little pastry cakes can be found in Sweden under the name of *Frijos* and in Norway where they are known as *Fattigman*.

Simple to prepare, these little fried pastries are excellent eaten mid-morning with coffee.

50g/2oz softened butter
175g/6oz soft pale brown sugar
450g/1lb plain flour
3 teaspoons baking powder
1 teaspoon cinnamon
1/2 teaspoon nutmeg

2 eggs, separated
300ml/1/2 pint milk

Topping
Icing sugar
Cinnamon

Preheat a deep fat fryer to 190°C/375°F.

Using an electric hand mixture, cream the butter and sugar until pale and fluffy.

Add the flour, baking powder, spices, egg yolks and milk a little at a time, mixing slowly until fully incorporated and completely smooth.

In a separate bowl whisk the egg whites until stiff and then gently fold them into the cake mixture, using a large metal spoon. If necessary add a little more flour to form a fairly stiff dough.

Lift the mixture out onto a lightly floured surface and knead gently for a moment before rolling out to about 1cm/1/2in thick. Cut the dough into strips about 7.5x5cm/3x2in and using a sharp knife cut a slit in the centre of each Cruller, pulling one end through the slit, to form a loose knot or alternatively cut three small slashes at an angle across each cake.

Fry the Crullers in the hot fat, for a couple of minutes on each side, by which time the cakes will be golden brown. Lift from the deep fryer using a slotted spoon and drain for a moment before resting them onto paper towelling to sprinkle with icing sugar and a little cinnamon. Traditionally eaten while still warm.

ALMOND ENVELOPES

DENMARK *Makes 4*

Almond envelopes are quite intriguing and absolutely delicious, filled with a raspberry preserve and a 'sausage' of almond paste and topped with flaked almonds.

¹/₂ batch of Danish pastry dough (page 20)

Filling
Raspberry purée
Almond paste

Topping
1 lightly beaten egg
Flaked almonds

Icing sugar

Preheat the oven to 190°C/375°F/Gas Mark 5.

Roll the dough out on a lightly floured surface and cut into 10x10cm/4x4in squares.

Spoon a teaspoon of raspberry purée into the centre of each square and top with a sausage of almond paste, about 5cm/2in long.

Pull two opposite corners of dough up over the filling pressing them together. Brush the pastries with lightly beaten egg and sprinkle with flaked almonds.

Lift onto two baking trays lined with greaseproof paper and bake in the oven for about 15-20 minutes or until golden brown. Be careful because they can cook quite quickly.

When baked, carefully lift onto a cooking rack and immediately sprinkle with the icing sugar. Allow to cool before eating.

TIPPALEIPA / MAY DAY PASTRIES

FINLAND

Makes 12

May Day celebrations in Finland are an important part of the calendar each year; the festivities include a large carnival and much drinking and eating including Tippaleipa, little crispy squiggles of fried pastry, which are accompanied by lemon mead, Sima.

7-10cm/3-4in sunflower oil	3 eggs, lightly beaten
275g/10oz plain flour	75ml/3fl oz beer
175g/6oz soft pale brown sugar	A little icing sugar to finish

Measure the oil into a deep fat fryer and heat to 180°C/350°F.

Sift the flour into a bowl, add the sugar and stir. Make a well in the centre and add the lightly beaten eggs. Using an electric hand mixer, slowly blend the ingredients together, gradually increasing the speed. Add the beer and blend to a smooth, lump free batter.

The best way to approach the next stage is to half fill a sturdy plastic bag with batter and cut a small hole in one of the bottom corners. Using this as a piping bag, drizzle a small amount of the batter into the hot fat, forming a snake-like coil about 10cm/4in in diameter.

Fry the Tippaleipa for a couple of minutes, turning over the pastries as they brown. When golden, lift out with a slotted spoon, allowing them to drain for a moment before placing onto a sheet of paper towel to remove any excess oil. Sprinkle with a little sifted icing sugar before eating.

KLAICHA / DATE PASTRIES

IRAQ   *Makes 12*

The profusion of dates in the Middle East has resulted in many ways of using them in their cakes and pastries. Klaichas are traditionally baked for the Eid celebrations (the end of fasting for Ramadan) and are perhaps one of the more typical. These little pastries are perfect for eating at any time of the day, accompanied by a cup of freshly brewed black coffee.

450g/1lb plain flour
50g/2oz soft pale brown sugar
225g/8oz butter
3 teaspoons rose water
50ml/2fl oz water

225g/8oz stoned dates
25g/1oz butter

Icing sugar

Sift the flour into a large bowl and stir in the sugar. Cut the butter into small pieces and rub it into the flour mix, using your fingertips. Add the rosewater and water and using a pallet knife, stir until it forms a ball of dough.

Wrap the dough in film and put it into the fridge to chill.

Meanwhile chop the dates into small pieces and cook them gently in the butter before setting aside to cool.

Preheat the oven to 180°C/350°F/Gas Mark 4. Break off a small piece of the dough, and roll into a ball about the size of a chestnut. On a lightly floured surface, flatten the ball into a circle and put a teaspoonful of the date mixture into the centre, before folding the cake in half to form a crescent shape. Repeat until all the date and dough mixtures have been used.

After putting the pastries onto the baking tray, put in the middle of the oven until golden brown, about 30 minutes. Remove from the baking tray and place on a wire cooling rack.

When completely cold, sprinkle lightly with a little sifted icing sugar.

DANISH PASTRIES / APRICOT STARS

DENMARK   *Makes 4*

It would be impossible to write about Danish cakes without mentioning Danish Pastries, which are now very popular the world over as, when freshly baked, they are hard to resist.

Various 'traditional' shapes include envelopes, snails, cock's combs, apricot slips, butter cakes, stars and crescents. Wonderfully fruity apricot stars, topped with a sticky glaze and glacé cherries, are perhaps one of my favourites. Often served at breakfast or at mid-morning with fresh coffee, they also go well with an afternoon cup of tea.

1/2 Batch of Danish pastry dough (page 20)

Filling
Apricot preserve

Topping
Lightly beaten egg

Decoration
Glacé cherries
Apricot glaze
Pinch of cardamom

Preheat the oven to 190°C/375°F/Gas Mark 5.

Place the dough onto a lightly floured surface and roll into a large square. Cut out as many squares 10x10cm/4x4in as possible.

Using a sharp knife cut a line from each corner of the square, into the centre, leaving an uncut area in the centre for the filling.

Place a generous teaspoonful of apricot preserve into the middle of the dough and pull a section from each corner into the centre, forming the pastries into a star shapes.

Brush the Danish Pastries with the lightly beaten egg, lift onto 2 baking trays lined with greaseproof paper.

Bake in the oven for about 15 minutes or until golden brown. Be careful because they can cook quite quickly.

In the meantime wash and chop the glacé cherries and when the pastries are baked, carefully lift onto a cooling rack and sprinkle with the cherries and brush with some apricot glaze. Allow to cool before eating.

BAKLAWA

Makes approx 30

Delicate sheets of filo pastry curl around the filling of ground nuts and orange flower water rather like little nests and once baked the Baklawas are steeped in wonderfully aromatic syrup.

450g/1lb filo pastry
115g/4oz butter, melted

Filling
2 egg whites
125g/4oz caster sugar
125g/4oz ground almonds
125g/4oz ground pistachios

125g/4oz ground walnuts
2 teaspoons orange flower water

Syrup
350g/12oz granulated sugar
425ml/15fl oz water
2 teaspoons fresh orange juice
2 teaspoons orange flower water

Liberally brush each of the sheets of filo pastry with melted butter, placing them on top of each other and covering with a damp cloth until required.

Whisk the egg whites and caster sugar until it stands in peaks and gently fold in the nuts and orange flower water.

Preheat the oven to 190°C/375°F/Gas Mark 5. Cut the sheets of filo into squares about 10cm/4in and taking a pile of 5 sheets of the little squares, place a tablespoonful of the nut filling into the centre and pull the sides of the pastry up to cup the filling but still allowing it to be visible in the centre. Repeat until all the little cakes have been made – there should be about 30 or a little more. Liberally butter two baking trays with sides and place the Baklawas on the trays being sure to place them close together which will help support the sides and retain the nest shape.

Bake the pastries in the oven for about 35 minutes, or until golden and crisp.

While the pastries are baking, put the sugar and water for the syrup into a small saucepan and slowly bring to the boil, stirring to dissolve the sugar. Allow to boil gently for about 10 minutes. Remove from the heat and stir in the orange juice and orange flower water.

When the cakes are baked, take them from the oven and leaving them on the trays, spoon over the syrup while they are still hot. Allow them to become cold before lifting onto a serving plate. They are delicious served with plain yogurt.

NEURIS

INDIA   *Makes 10-12*

These pastry squares are always among the little cakes baked for the Hindu festival of Diwali. It is celebrated with all manner of aromatic sweetmeats, served to guests and family members but also often given as gifts. The fillings vary according to family preferences, but the recipe given below is very typical.

Filling

60g/2¹/2oz soft pale brown sugar
115g/4oz desiccated coconut
25g/1oz pistachio nuts, chopped
25g/1oz almonds, chopped
25g/1oz sultanas, chopped
250ml/9fl oz evaporated milk
¹/2 teaspoon ground mace
¹/2 teaspoon ground cinnamon

10-12 sheets filo pastry
115g/4oz butter, melted
(or more if necessary)

Topping
Desiccated coconut

Measure the sugar, coconut, pistachio nuts, almonds, sultanas, evaporated milk and spices, into a small saucepan and gently bring to the boil, stirring constantly. Turn to a low heat and allow the ingredients to simmer for about 8-9 minutes, stirring occasionally, by which time the filling will have thickened. Set the pan aside to cool.

Preheat the oven to 180°C/350°F/Gas Mark 4. Take a sheet of the filo pastry and brush with some melted butter, fold the filo in half and repeat until the pastry is approximately 15x15cm/6x6in. Place a couple of generous teaspoonfuls of the filling onto one half of the pastry and after damping the filo edges, pull the other half of the pastry over the filling and press the edges firmly together.

Finally, place the cakes onto 2 baking sheets, greased and lined with baking paper and dampen the tops with a little more melted butter and sprinkle with the desiccated coconut.

Bake in the oven for about 20-25 minutes or until lightly puffed and golden brown. Lift onto a cooling rack and leave to become cold before serving.

KONAFA, KATAIFI AND K'NAFI JIBNA / GROUND NUT PASTRIES

GULF STATES

Makes 12

Coffee has a prominent place in an Arab's life; always strong, dark and aromatic it is served in small cups, which are regularly filled from beautifully ornate coffee pots. It is considered very rude to your host to refuse a second or even a third cup but when the guest gently swivels their cup from side to side, this is an indication that they do not want anymore to drink.

Sweet, sticky and aromatic cakes such as Konafa, made from finely shredded pastry and known under several names, are often served with coffee. It is however, very difficult to make without the right equipment, as the shreds of pastry are very fine and almost impossible to cut thinly enough by hand. But this shredded filo pastry can often now be found in Middle Eastern food shops, so do go and ask.

Pastry
450g/1lb Konafa pastry
225g/8oz butter, melted

Filling
125g/4oz ground almonds
125g/4oz ground walnuts
125g/4oz caster sugar
1/2 teaspoon ground mace
1/2 teaspoon cinnamon
1/2 teaspoon ground clove

1 egg white, lightly whisked
1 tablespoon lemon juice

Syrup
375g/12oz granulated sugar
425ml/15fl oz water
1 tablespoon lemon juice
Zest of a lemon
3 whole cloves
1/2 cinnamon stick
2 tablespoons honey

Preheat the oven to 180°C/350°F/Gas Mark 4. On a lightly floured cool surface, unroll some of the Konafa pastry, laying the strands out to form a rectangle about 18x25cm/7x10in and brush liberally with the melted butter.

Weigh all the filling ingredients into a bowl and stir together thoroughly. Spoon some of the filling along the shortest edge of the pastry strands and tightly roll into a 'sausage'. Repeat this until all the strands and filling have been used.

Carefully lift each of the long rolls onto a well buttered 20x30cm/8x12in baking tray, leaving very little space between them to lend support as they cook and place the tray into the centre of the oven. After about 45 minutes check that the cakes are golden brown and crisp. They can be left a little longer if you feel they are not quite cooked.

Meanwhile in a small saucepan, heat the sugar and water, stirring steadily until the syrup boils and the sugar has dissolved. Add the lemon juice, zest, cloves and cinnamon stick and bring the syrup to the boil, turn the heat down and allow it to simmer for about 10 minutes. Remove from the heat and stir in the honey before setting the saucepan aside to cool.

When the tray of pastries are cooked, remove from the oven and pour the cooled syrup evenly over all the pastries before setting aside to get completely cold. When cold, cut the pastries evenly into smaller cakes and serve with strong black coffee.

OZNEI HAMAN

ISRAEL   *Makes 8*

These three-cornered pastry cakes are traditionally eaten at Purim, the festival celebrating the failure of the evil Haman in exterminating the Jews of Persia. Haman wore a triangular hat, which is represented by the shape of the little cakes.

Fillings do vary but perhaps the most popular and widely recognised are poppy seeds and honey or apricot purée. Each family would appear to have their own favourite recipe but having tried several I think this simple version gives excellent results.

Dough
150g/5oz softened butter
150g/5oz caster sugar
1 teaspoon vanilla extract
2 eggs
275g/10oz plain flour

Filling
50g/2oz poppy seeds
50g/2oz chopped raisins

50g/2oz grated apple
1 tablespoon honey
50g/2oz caster sugar
75ml/3fl oz water
Zest of a lemon
1 tablespoon lemon juice
50g/2oz ground almonds
1 egg

A little beaten egg for sealing

Cream the butter and sugar until light and fluffy, stir in the vanilla extract and beat in the eggs and flour, a little at a time, until a dough forms. Transfer to a lightly floured surface and knead gently until smooth. Wrap in cling film and place into the refrigerator.

In a small saucepan, measure the poppy seeds, raisins, apple, honey, sugar, water and the zest and lemon juice, bring the filling to the boil stirring until well mixed. Remove from the heat and continue to beat while adding the ground almonds and egg. Allow to cool.

Preheat the oven to 180°C/350°F/Gas Mark 4. Roll out the dough on a lightly floured surface and cut into circles approximately 7.5cm/3in diameter, pressing out as many rounds as possible. Spoon 2 teaspoonfuls of the filling into the centre of each cake round and brush the edges with the beaten egg. Bring the sides of the dough up to the centre, forming a tricorne shape. Lift onto 2 baking trays lined with greaseproof paper, brush the tops with a little egg before cooking in the centre of the oven for about 25 minutes or until golden brown.

Allow to cool slightly before transferring to a wire rack to become cold.

M'HANNCHA / SERPENT CAKE

MOROCCO   *Serves 8-10*

One of the most popular of the Moroccan pastries, the name M'hanncha means 'the snake' and it is not hard to see how it acquired its name; the almond cake closely resembling a coiled reptile.

I didn't find it easy to prepare but a little practice made perfect (well almost) and it was absolutely delicious.

225g/8oz ground almonds	8 sheets filo pastry
175g/6oz icing sugar	6 tablespoons melted butter
1/2 teaspoon almond extract	
1 egg yolk, beaten	**To dust**
1 tablespoon orange flower water	Icing sugar
	Cinnamon powder

Preheat the oven to 180°C/350°F/Gas Mark 4.

Place the almonds, icing sugar, almond extract, egg yolk and orange flower water into a bowl and knead together to form a soft dough. The orange flower water helps to prevent oils leaking from the ground almonds. Divide into 4 pieces. Dust a worktop lightly with icing sugar, roll each piece into long sausage shapes about 1.5cm/3/4in thick. Set aside and chill.

Place a sheet of filo onto the worktop and brush liberally with melted butter; place a second sheet on top and brush again with the butter. Put one of the almond 'sausages' onto the pastry and carefully roll up tightly. Cover with a damp cloth and repeat the procedure with the remaining 6 sheets of pastry and 3 almond sausages.

Finally lift one of the 'sausages' onto a large, well greased baking tray and shape into a coil, following with the other three, giving one large coiled 'snake'. Brush generously with the remaining butter and place into the hot oven for 25-30 minutes until golden brown.

Remove from the oven and using a second greased baking sheet, carefully invert the snake and replace into the oven for a further 10 minutes to allow the underside to cook.

Finally remove from the oven and slide onto a large serving plate. Allow to cool slightly before dusting with the icing sugar and cinnamon. Best eaten while slightly warm.

KAAB EL GHAZAL / GAZELLE'S HORNS

MOROCCO   *Makes 8*

One of the most popular of all the Moroccan pastries, no wedding or celebration feast would be complete without Gazelle's Horns. Utterly delectable, the delicate flavour of orange flower water contrasts wonderfully well with ground almonds and just a little practice will enable you to perfect these traditional delicacies.

Filling

250g/9oz ground almonds

115g/4oz icing sugar

2 tablespoons orange flower water

25g/1oz butter, melted

1 egg white, gently beaten

A generous pinch of ground cinnamon

Pastry

300g/10oz plain flour

25g/1oz butter, melted

1 egg yolk

2 tablespoons orange flower water

Place all the ingredients for the filling in a bowl and begin kneading them until the warmth from your hands releases the oil from the ground almonds. Once a smooth dough has formed put to one side while you begin to make the pastry.

Preheat the oven 180°C/350°F/Gas Mark 4. Sift the flour into a bowl and add the remaining pastry ingredients. Knead for about 5 minutes or until the dough becomes smooth and elastic (a little water may be added if the mix is felt to be too dry). On a lightly floured surface, roll out the pastry as thinly as possible, to form a rectangular shape. Neaten the edges before cutting into 7.5x7.5cm/3x3in squares. Taking a walnut sized piece of the filling, roll it to form a sausage shape, thicker in the centre and tapered at the ends, about 6cm/2½in long. Place one into the centre of each of the squares, until the entire filling and pastry has been used. Dampen the edges of the pastry before gently pulling the front edge over the filling and sealing the edges. Using a pastry wheel cut and crimp the edges before gently pulling the little pastries into crescent shapes.

Lift carefully onto a lightly oiled baking tray and bake for about 15-20 minutes until pale brown.

Remove and carefully lift onto cooling racks, before sifting with a little icing sugar. Excellent eaten warm but equally good when cold – if there are any left!

BRIOUATES

These intriguing little pastries are often served in Moroccan households, coming with a variety of sweet fillings, commonly dates and figs, almonds and honey or fresh fruits, and occasionally, savoury fillings of cheese or minced lamb. While they are normally baked using a delicate pastry named yufka or warkha, it is quite possible to use filo with great effect, particularly as this is widely available from all good supermarkets and delicatessens.

100g/4oz butter	12 sheets filo pastry
100g/4oz dates, finely chopped	120g/4oz butter, melted
100g/4oz soft dried figs, finely chopped	1 egg yolk, beaten
2 tablespoons orange flower water	
2 tablespoons ground almonds	4 tablespoons melted honey
	Icing sugar

Melt the butter gently in a medium saucepan, adding the dates and figs, stir for a moment before adding the orange flower water and ground almonds. Remove from the heat and stir together thoroughly, before putting into a food processor and pulverising for a moment to a smooth paste. Allow the mixture to cool a little and spoon out into a clean bowl.

Meanwhile on a very lightly floured surface place the sheets of filo pastry on top of each other liberally brushing each sheet with the melted butter and cut into strips approximately 10cm/4in wide. Using one strip of pastry at a time, place a dessertspoonful of the filling onto the dough and fold in into triangles by folding to the right and then the left, the end of the dough being sealed with a little of the egg yolk.

Place the Briouate to one side and continue until all the pastry and filling has been used.

Using a saucepan with a little shallow oil, fry the Briouates two or three at a time, turning them over frequently until lightly browned, this should take about 5 or 6 minutes at the most.

Finally using a slotted spoon to allow them to drain, lift the fried pastries out onto a large plate and when you have cooked all the Briouates drizzle them with a little of the melted honey, or if preferred decorate with sifted icing sugar. Serve while fresh.

MOON CAKES

CHINA   *Makes 2*

Knowing that I was working on a new cake book, Kate Hart, who bakes with me brought in a Moon Cake, which a relative had given her. Beautifully presented in a box decorated with Chinese symbols, cutting it in half revealed a 'moon' – a perfectly cooked egg yolk baked in the centre of a ground nut filling encased in a glazed pastry case. Then Anna McNamee with whom I did a Radio 4 series on cakes and whose mother is Chinese told me that Moon Cakes in northern China have only two kinds of fillings, white sugar paste or brown date paste, while those in the south have a large variety of fillings from ham, dates or preserved apricots to walnuts and watermelon seeds.

I also discovered how in the 14th century, the Chinese peasants rose up against the tyrannical Mongolians. During the Autumn Moon Festival messages were hidden inside these little cakes, detailing where and when the uprising would take place. It was subsequently a success and so to this day those cakes have continued to be central to the Moon festivities with specialist bakers more usually preparing them. However, this slightly simplified version, which may be baked at home, made with red adzuki beans (available from Chinese food stores) or ground almonds, is well worth trying.

2 eggs	**Filling**
Pastry	225g/8oz red adzuki bean paste
225g/8oz plain flour	
90g/3oz butter	**Glaze**
90g/3oz lard	Beaten egg
30g/1oz caster sugar	
Approx 150ml/¼ pint cold water	

Boil the 2 eggs for 10 minutes. Remove from heat and run under cold water before removing the shell and then carefully cutting the white of the egg away, to leave you with two whole yolks, set aside to become completely cold.

Preheat the oven to 180°C/350°F/Gas Mark 4. Measure the flour, butter and lard into a bowl and rub in with your fingertips until it resembles breadcrumbs. Stir in the sugar before making a well in the centre, and stirring with a knife, add the water a little at a time until a ball is formed. Knead gently on a lightly floured surface until the dough is smooth. Divide the dough into two before cutting both halves into pieces of two-thirds and a third. Set the smaller pieces aside to use as lids later.

Roll the two larger portions into circles large enough to fill each of two 10cm/4in loose bottom pie tins when dropped carefully in and pressed firmly against the sides. Fill each pastry base to half way with adzuki bean paste, before placing the egg yolk into the centre of each and filling the moulds to the top with the remaining adzuki paste.

Finally, roll the two remaining portions of pastry into circles large enough to cover the top of the pies, damping the edges to seal and trimming away surplus pastry before brushing lightly with a little beaten egg.

Place the pies onto a baking sheet and cook for 25-30 minutes, or until golden brown.

Allow to cool for 20-30 minutes before sliding them out of their tins. Leave to become completely cold before eating.

Note: I find the best way to slide cakes/pies from a loose bottomed tin, is to stand them on a jam jar (or something similar), allowing the tin to drop down from around the pie. They can then be easily lifted onto a cooling rack.

APRICOT EMPANADITAS

MEXICO   *Makes 16*

These very simple little puff pastry cakes are delicious and easy to prepare. You will find the recipe for puff pastry on page 18 but you will certainly be forgiven for buying it ready made.

450g/1lb puff pastry   A generous pinch of cinnamon
225g/8oz apricot jam   50g/2oz ground almonds
50g/2oz flaked almonds

Preheat the oven to 190°C/375°F/Gas Mark 5. On a lightly floured board, roll out the pastry to a square approximately 30x30cm/12x12in and then cut it into equally sized portions, about 7½cm/3in.

Mix the jam, flaked almonds and cinnamon together in a small bowl, before spooning an equal amount into the centre of each pastry square. Wet the edges with a little water and fold over the pastry to form triangles. Lift them onto a lightly greased baking tray allowing space in between each cake for them to puff up.

Bake in the centre of the oven until golden brown and well puffed, about 15-20 minutes, being careful not to over cook.

When baked, lift them onto a wire cooling rack and immediately sprinkle with ground almonds. Allow to cool a little before eating, as the jam in the centre will be very hot.

MELKTERT CAKE / MILK TART CAKE

SOUTH AFRICA

Brought to South Africa by the Dutch, this extremely popular cake is served in the afternoon with tea or coffee although I admit I found the idea of a 'milk tart' very bland. However, when I baked one, it was easy to see why it is one of South Africa's favourite teatime cakes.

Pastry
175g/6oz self-raising flour
75g/3oz butter, grated
75g/3oz caster sugar
1 egg yolk
A little cold water

50g/2oz butter
50g/2oz plain flour
25g/1oz cornflour
75g/3oz caster sugar
2 eggs, beaten
1 teaspoon vanilla extract
A little ground cinnamon if liked

Filling
600ml/1 pint cold milk

Icing sugar to dust top

Measure the flour into a bowl and add the grated butter, stir with a pallet knife. Add the sugar, egg yolk and enough cold water to form a stiff dough. Knead lightly until smooth, wrap in film and set aside in the refrigerator while you prepare the filling.

Measure the milk, butter, flour, cornflour and caster sugar into a medium saucepan and place over a low heat, whisking constantly until the milk boils and the mixture thickens. Remove from the heat and beat in the two eggs a little at a time and finally the vanilla extract.

Preheat the oven to 180°C/350°F/Gas Mark 4. Remove the pastry from the refrigerator, roll out on a lightly floured surface and line a 20cm/8in tart tin. Pour in the filling, sprinkling lightly with ground cinnamon and place in the centre of the preheated oven, baking for about 25 minutes.

Leave to become cold. Before serving lightly dust with a little sifted icing sugar.

ÉCLAIRS

Makes 6

For some reason, éclairs are always seen as difficult to cook, but that is really not the case. As long as you follow the recipe carefully they can be prepared quite quickly and cooked as oblongs or small balls which are filled with cream and dipped into chocolate.

50g/2oz butter	60g/2¹/2 oz plain flour
150ml/1/4 pint water	2 eggs, lightly beaten

Preheat the oven to 200°C/400°F/Gas Mark 6. Melt the butter in a saucepan with the water, bringing it to the boil.

Remove the saucepan from the heat and quickly beat in the flour, I find it best to use a wooden spoon. Continue beating until the mixture becomes smooth and shiny and forms a ball. Allow the mixture to cool slightly.

Add the eggs a little at a time and continuing to beat, keep the éclair mixture together. Watch carefully, adding just enough egg, as we want the mixture to be able to hold its shape.

Using a forcing bag and plain nozzle, pipe the cake mixture into oblongs of about 10cm/4in. onto a lightly greased baking tray. Bake in the centre of the oven for about 20-25 minutes or until golden brown and crisp. Remove them from the oven and transfer them to a wire cooling rack. Using a sharp knife, slit a hole in the side of the éclairs to allow the steam out, otherwise they will become soft.

Once cold fill with whipped cream and if liked dip the tops into some melted chocolate, placing them back onto the wire rack to dry.

SPICED CAKES

Cakes all over the world have greatly benefited from the use of spices from India, China and Indonesia; ginger and cinnamon for example are so much a part of Britain's range of gingerbreads such as Parkin. The black pepper, cinnamon and nutmeg used in Holland to flavour Kruidkoek produces a sensationally spicy cake and who would think of baking a fruit cake without the wonderful background taste and aroma of mixed spice?

The cakes of the Mediterranean and North Africa are usually baked with wonderfully warm, mellow spices such as mace, cardamom, nutmeg, cloves and cinnamon, whereas the cakes of Northern Europe and Scandinavia are often more plain but include flavourings such as poppy seed.

The spice trade was a dangerous but lucrative one; the Romans used spices in almost all their dishes and their ships heavily laden with spice, ploughed their way to Egypt, where they found the ancient Egyptians using spices to flavour and preserve their food as well as for cosmetics and for aromatherapy. Wherever the Romans went, spices went with them to areas of the world which had previously known little about them, Europe included. As it could take two to three years to sail a round trip, it is easy to see why spices were expensive and a symbol of wealth and power and hence became so important.

From the 15th to the 18th century the Portuguese, the Dutch and the English became the great spice trading nations but it was the Spanish who discovered and traded one of the few spices indigenous to the New World, vanilla, which has now become such an essential ingredient in cakes the world over.

KERMAKAKKU / SOUR CREAM CAKE

FINLAND

Traditionally baked in a loaf tin, this wonderfully light cake is delectably aromatic, containing mace, cinnamon and cardamom – it varies slightly between bakers. Like so many Scandinavian cakes the tin is coated with butter and dried breadcrumbs, giving it a crunchy finish.

25g/1oz softened butter	1 heaped teaspoon bicarbonate of soda
2 tablespoons dried breadcrumbs	1 teaspoon mace
	1 teaspoon cinnamon
115g/4oz butter	1 teaspoon cardamom
225g/8oz caster sugar	3 eggs, lightly beaten
225g/8oz self-raising flour	180ml/6fl oz sour cream

Coat the inside of a 900g/2lb loaf tin with the softened butter and spoon in the dried breadcrumbs, tilting the tin to cover the inside and tipping out any surplus.

Preheat the oven to 180°C/350°F/Gas Mark 4.

Cream the butter and sugar together until pale and fluffy. In a separate bowl sift together the flour, bicarbonate of soda and spices.

Slowly add the spiced flour, eggs and sour cream a little at a time to the creamed butter and sugar, ensuring they are of a smooth consistency.

Spoon the mixture into the prepared loaf tin and bake for about 1 hour, or until the cake is pale golden brown and springy to touch.

Remove the cake from the oven and allow it to stand for about 10 minutes before placing a rack over the top of the tin and shaking it gently to release the cake from its tin. Carefully turn the cake the right way up and leave it to cool before eating.

PUMPKIN CAKE

INDIA

A beautifully spiced cake, with a soft texture, Pumpkin Cake is eaten all over India with recipes having been passed down through families. It is certainly well worth trying.

450g/1lb cooked and mashed pumpkin
350g/12oz soft pale brown sugar
300ml/ 1/2 pint sunflower oil
3 eggs
450g/1lb plain flour

1 teaspoon baking powder
1 teaspoon cinnamon
1 teaspoon nutmeg
1 teaspoon mace

Preheat the oven to 180°C/350°F/Gas Mark 4.

Weigh the pumpkin and sugar into a blender and whiz together until smooth. Add the sunflower oil and eggs and blend for a further 2 or 3 minutes until completely smooth.

In a large bowl sift together the flour, baking powder and spices. Make a well in the centre and pour in the pumpkin mixture, stirring well together until completely combined.

Pour into a greased and lined 18cm/7in square cake tin and bake in the centre of the oven for about 1 hour or a little longer, until the cake is golden brown and feels springy when pressed in the centre.

Remove the cake from the oven and leave for about 10 minutes before lifting out onto a cooling rack and carefully peeling off the greaseproof paper. Leave to become completely cold before cutting into squares. The cake may be sprinkled with a little sifted icing sugar if liked.

POPPY SEED CAKE

RUSSIA

Widely used in Russia, poppy seeds are wonderfully aromatic, their flavour enhancing both cakes and bread; the end products are always very good with strong dark coffee.

125g/4oz poppy seeds, crushed	225g/8oz soft pale brown sugar
300ml/1/2 pint milk	4 eggs, separated
	350g/12oz self-raising flour
225g/8oz softened butter	1 teaspoon baking powder

Measure the poppy seeds into the milk in a small saucepan and bring to the boil, before setting it aside to become completely cold.

Preheat the oven to 160°C/325°F/Gas Mark 3. Using an electric hand mixer, cream together the butter and sugar, until light and fluffy.

Slowly add the egg yolks, flour and baking powder a little at a time, constantly mixing on low speed. Finally mix in the poppy seeded milk.

In a clean bowl whisk the egg whites until stiff, before folding them into the cake mixture.

Spoon the cake into a greased 900g/2lb loaf tin and place into the centre of the oven. Bake for about an hour, or until the cake is well risen, golden and springy to touch. Leave for about 10 minutes to cool slightly before turning out onto a cooling rack.

KRUIDKOEK / SPICE CAKE

HOLLAND

This particular recipe for Kruidkoek contains lots of cinnamon, cloves, nutmeg and a generous amount of black pepper and is a wonderfully spiced cake.

275g/10oz plain flour	1/2 teaspoon ground mace
225g/8oz soft dark muscovado sugar	1/2 teaspoon ground black pepper
4 teaspoons baking powder	50g/2oz ground ginger
4 teaspoons ground cinnamon	115g/4oz butter, melted
1 teaspoon ground nutmeg	150ml/1/4 pint milk

Preheat the oven to 150°C/300°F/Gas Mark 2.

Measure all the ingredients into a large bowl and using an electric hand mixer, whisk them together on a low speed, ensuring the cake mix is lump free.

Pour the cake mixture into a greased and lined 18cm/7in cake tin and place in the centre of the oven, baking for about 1 hour. When the cake feels firm to touch and a skewer inserted into the centre comes out cleanly, remove from the oven and leave the cake to cool.

After 20 minutes remove the cake from its tin and transfer to a cooling rack.

LOVE CAKE

SRI LANKA

Passed down through families, the recipe for a Love Cake is thought to have originated from the Portuguese who once ruled Ceylon. Each recipe varies a little, so it really is possible to choose which you prefer. It should be cooked quite slowly, so that while the outer edges are firm, the centre remains really moist, rather like chocolate brownies.

6 large eggs	1/2 teaspoon ground cardamom
450g/1lb caster sugar	1/2 teaspoon ground nutmeg
175g/6oz softened butter	1/2 teaspoon ground cloves
3 tablespoons honey	1/2 teaspoon cinnamon
2 tablespoons rosewater	250g/8oz semolina
Grated zest of lemon	250g/8oz chopped cashew nuts
1/2 teaspoon ground mace	250g/8oz chopped glacé pineapple

Preheat the oven to 150°C/300°F/Gas Mark 2.

Using a hand mixer on high speed, whisk the eggs and sugar together until pale and thick enough to leave a trail when the beaters are held above the mixture.

Add the softened butter, honey, rosewater, lemon zest, spices and semolina beating on the lowest speed until fully mixed together. Finally stir in the chopped cashew nuts and glacé pineapple.

Line a 25x30cm/10x12in cake tin with 2 layers of greaseproof paper and spoon in the mixture, smoothing the surface lightly before putting into the centre of the preheated oven.

Bake for about 45 minutes until the top is golden brown.

When completely cold, turn the cake out of the tin and gently peel off the greaseproof paper.

Cut into squares to serve.

PARKIN

YORKSHIRE, ENGLAND

In keeping with its Celtic connections, Parkin is also known as Thor, Tharf or Thar Cake.

It is wonderfully dark and spicy and was originally eaten at Celtic or Christian festivals, although it is now traditionally served around the bonfire on Guy Fawkes' night. It has always been more popular in the north of England where it is made with coarse oatmeal and black treacle. Best baked at least a week ahead, by which time it will have become soft and sticky, it should be cut into squares before serving.

225g/8oz plain wholemeal flour	175g /6oz dark muscovado sugar
1 teaspoon bicarbonate of soda	115g/4oz butter
2 teaspoons ground ginger	50g/2oz golden syrup
1 teaspoon cinnamon	115g/4oz black treacle
1 teaspoon mixed spice	150ml/5fl oz milk
1/2 teaspoon salt	1 large egg
100g/4oz coarse oatmeal	

Preheat the oven to 180°C/350°F/Gas Mark 4.

Sift the flour, bicarbonate of soda, spices and salt into a large bowl. Stir in the oatmeal and sugar, making a well in the centre.

In a medium saucepan melt the butter, syrup and treacle over a low heat and then set aside to cool slightly before adding to the dry ingredients. Beat the milk and egg together in a jug and pour into the mixture, ensuring that you continue beating to eliminate any lumps that may form.

Immediately pour into a greased and lined 20cm/8in square cake tin and put it into the centre of the oven and bake for about 50 minutes or until firm to touch.

Allow to cool slightly before turning out onto a wire rack to become cold, when it should be wrapped in greaseproof paper and foil.

Stored in a cool dry place to mellow, the cake will also change in texture, becoming sticky and inviting.

MELOMAKARONA /
SPICED HONEY CAKES

CYPRUS
Makes 10

Spices such as cinnamon, cloves, nutmeg and coriander appear in many Cypriot recipes and there is a prolific harvest of oranges, mandarins, tangerines, limes, lemons and grapefruits as well as an abundance of walnut and almonds, all of which find their way into these festive cakes. Surprisingly the English have influenced the food eaten in some strange ways; I was amused to learn that at Christmas most Cypriot homes will have a traditional English Christmas Cake as well as these little buns which are baked for both unexpected callers and of course, the family.

Dough
225g/8oz butter
225g/8oz caster sugar
Zest of a lemon
Zest of an orange
150ml/1/4 pint corn oil
2 tablespoons Cointreau or brandy
450g/1lb plain flour
4 level teaspoons baking powder
1/4 teaspoon ground cloves
1/4 teaspoon ground cinnamon
1/4 teaspoon ground nutmeg

Filling
1/4 teaspoon ground cinnamon
2 tablespoons honey
1 tablespoon Cointreau or brandy
175g/6oz ground walnuts

Syrup
250ml/9fl oz water
Juice of a lemon
Juice of an orange
175g/6oz granulated sugar
4 tablespoons honey

Cream the butter and caster sugar together in a large bowl, add the zest of the lemon and the orange and stir thoroughly. Pour in the corn oil, Cointreau or brandy and sift in the flour, baking powder and spices, stirring or using your hands knead gently to form a dough. Wrap in cling film and place into the refrigerator while you make the filling and prepare the syrup.

Place all the filling ingredients into a small bowl and stir until they come together.

Place all the syrup ingredients into a small saucepan and set aside.

Preheat the oven to 180°C/350°F/Gas Mark 4. Remove the dough from the cling film and on a lightly floured surface break off a small amount, about the size of a plum, and flatten it gently. Spoon a small amount of the filling into the centre of the dough circle and seal the edges over the top, to form an oval shape. Turn them upside down when placing them onto two baking trays lined with greaseproof paper and make a pattern with the prongs of a fork.

Bake in the centre of the oven for about 20-25 minutes until golden brown. Cool on a wire rack.

Heat the syrup to boiling point, stirring until dissolved, and leave to simmer for about 9-10 minutes. Finally using a slotted spoon, dip each of the Honey Cakes into the simmering syrup, turning several times before lifting out onto the wire rack and allowing to become cold.

SPICED CAKES   147

RAS-EL-HANOUT SPICED FRUIT CAKE

MOROCCO

Ras-el-Hanout Spiced Fruit Cake is a wonderful example of the importance of spices in Moroccan cookery and I simply could not resist including it because of the type of spices used to add flavour to this really delicious cake. Ras-el-Hanout means 'Head of the Shop' or 'Top of the Shop' and this unique Moroccan spice is quite simply a mixture of the shopkeeper's favourite spices, ranging from coriander, nutmeg, cloves, cardamom, cinnamon, ginger and nutmeg to the flowers of lavender and rosebuds. This mixture can now be found among the larger ranges of spices from delicatessens and supermarkets, so it is worth searching for.

The cake itself is also rather different as the fruits are steeped in Earl Grey tea overnight. The day before baking, measure out the following fruits:

75g/3oz raisins	75g/3oz currants
75g/3oz ready to eat dried apricots	250ml/10fl oz boiling water
75g/3oz ready to eat prunes	2 Earl Grey teabags
75g/3oz sultanas	

Cut the raisins, apricots and prunes into small pieces and combine in a bowl with the sultanas and currants. Pour the boiling water onto the teabags and stir. After 10 minutes remove the bags and pour the tea onto the fruits, stirring thoroughly and setting aside to leave the fruit to absorb the tea. Cover and leave overnight.

225g/8oz self-raising flour	150g/5oz soft pale brown sugar
2 level teaspoons Ras-el-Hanout	1 egg, lightly beaten

Preheat the oven to 180°C/350°F/Gas Mark 4. Sift the flour and spice together and stir in the sugar. Add the fruit mixture and the beaten egg and stir until all the ingredients are completely incorporated. If necessary a little milk may be added to give a dropping consistency. Spoon the cake mix into a 900g/2lb loaf tin with greaseproof liner and bake in the centre of the oven for about an hour until well risen and firm to touch. Check with a skewer to ensure it is cooked right through. Allow the cake to cool slightly before gently turning out onto a wire cooling rack.

SHOOFLY CAKE

PENNSYLVANIA, USA

Shoofly Cake is bursting with enough flavour to 'Shoo away the flies', which is apparently the way this cake is regarded in America. I have also found recipes for Shoofly Cup Cakes and Shoofly Pie so the rich spicy taste clearly has a lot of fans.

450g/1lb plain wholemeal flour
175g/6oz dark molasses sugar
1/2 teaspoon ground cinnamon
1/2 teaspoon ground ginger
1/2 teaspoon ground nutmeg
1 teaspoon baking powder
1 teaspoon cream of tartar
115g/4oz butter

1 teaspoon baking soda
300ml/1/2 pint very hot water
350g/12oz molasses syrup
1 large egg, lightly beaten

Topping
50g/2oz fresh breadcrumbs
1/2 teaspoon ground cinnamon

Preheat the oven to 190°C/375°F/Gas Mark 5. In a medium bowl, stir together the flour, sugar, cinnamon, ginger, nutmeg, baking powder and cream of tartar. Using your fingertips, rub in the butter until it has the consistency of fine breadcrumbs. Make a well in the centre of the mixture and set to one side.

In a separate bowl, stir the baking soda in the hot water, adding the molasses syrup and stirring until completely dissolved. Pour the mixture into the centre of the flour mix, adding the lightly beaten egg. Stir well until all the ingredients form a smooth, thick batter.

Pour the cake mixture into a greased shallow cake tin, 15x15cm/6x6in and sprinkle the breadcrumbs and cinnamon over the top of the cake. Bake in the centre of the preheated oven for about 25-30 minutes or until the cake feels springy to touch.

Turn the cake out onto a cooling rack and leave to become completely cold.

PEPPARKAKSDEG / GINGERBREAD HOUSE

SWEDEN

Grimm's fairytale Hansel and Gretel was probably the first reference to gingerbread houses as part of Christmas festivities. Prior to that, only cookies cut into animal shapes and figures were found in the markets and towns of Northern Europe and Scandinavia.

It was a Swedish friend, Llynne who first introduced me to them as she made them for her children every year. An artistically built, beautifully decorated house can be found in most Swedish and German homes at Christmas together with a 'Tomte' the benevolent elf which sits on the family table eating his porridge – he smiles sweetly but woe betide you if you neglect him. In our house we are actually rather scared not to put him on the Christmas table!

If you have young children they will really enjoy preparing and building a gingerbread house and you will be surprised how quickly it becomes part of your Christmas.

115g/4oz butter	1 teaspoon ground cinnamon
115g/4oz pale muscovado sugar	
1 egg, lightly beaten	**Decorations**
4 tablespoons black treacle	185g/6oz glacé icing
400g/14oz self-raising flour	A variety of small colourful sweets
2 teaspoons ground ginger	Silver balls and sugar flowers

Cream the butter and sugar in a large bowl until light and fluffy. Add the lightly beaten egg together with the black treacle, flour and spices. The mixture will be stiff and you may need to gather it together by hand, kneading it lightly. Place in a polythene bag and chill for about an hour.

Preheat the oven to 180°C/350°F/Gas Mark 4. Roll the dough out on a lightly floured board and using the template drawn on page 256, cut out the shapes and transfer carefully onto lightly greased baking trays.

Place in the oven and bake for about 15 minutes until risen and brown. Allow to cool slightly before transferring to a cooling rack. Place icing in a piping bag and 'glue' the sections together, adding the sweets for decorations.

LARGE CAKES

The cakes in this section are a real pot pourri; often simply rather different and not easy to categorise.

One truly outstanding cake is Norwegian Kransekake, which is very difficult to make. About sixteen almond meringue rings are piped onto greaseproof paper, the rings gradually decreasing in size, beginning with a 25cm/10in and finishing with a 5cm/2in ring. The layers are then built up with squiggles of white icing and decorated with flowers, ribbons or little Norwegian flags. The finished cake is an incredibly impressive centrepiece.

Not all the cakes in this section are so difficult though, the carrot cake for example is easy to bake, easy to decorate and definitely easy to eat.

Another great cake is the Canadian Tomato Soup Cake – it not only tastes good – it makes people smile, which must be a good reason to bake one.

A cake which is not only great for tea time but flexible enough to serve as a pudding is the Austrian Viennese Curd Cake, and it is certainly well worth the time taken to prepare. I guarantee you will be rewarded for your efforts – it is delicious.

BOILED FRUIT CAKE

IRELAND

Southern Ireland has a long history of teatime cakes, the Irish being quite rightly very proud of their simple, homely cooking. I have chosen this boiled fruit cake because it is a wonderful example of the depth of flavour it is possible to put into everyday baking. It is incidentally, excellent sliced and buttered or served with Irish Cheddar cheese.

150g/5oz butter	225g/8oz plain flour
150g/5oz soft dark brown sugar	1 teaspoon baking powder
115g/4oz sultanas	1 teaspoon bicarbonate of soda
115g/4oz currants	2 teaspoons mixed spice
115g/4oz raisins	2 large eggs
50g/2oz chopped mixed peel	

Preheat the oven to 150°C/300°/Gas Mark 2.

Put the butter, sugar, dried fruits and peel into a saucepan together with about 250ml/9fl oz of water and bring to the boil, stirring occasionally. Leave to simmer for 15 minutes. Set aside to cool before adding the flour, baking powder, bicarbonate of soda, spice and eggs, stirring well to ensure all the ingredients are fully incorporated.

Spoon the mixture into a buttered and lined 18cm/7in cake tin and bake in the centre of the preheated oven for about 1½ hours or until springy to touch and golden brown. When the cake is quite cold, remove from the tin, wrap in another sheet of greaseproof and store in an airtight container.

This cake will taste even better if left a day or two before eating.

LINZERTORTE / RASPBERRY CAKE

AUSTRIA

At first a Linzertorte may just look like a raspberry tart but it is a luscious cake, produced by creaming butter and sugar, adding an egg, flour, spices and ground almonds before finally topping with fresh raspberries.

115g/4oz softened butter	½ teaspoon ground cloves
115g/4oz caster sugar	150g/5oz ground almonds
1 egg	350g/12oz fresh raspberries
175/6oz plain flour	A little sugar
½ teaspoon ground cinnamon	

Using a hand held mixer, cream the butter and sugar until thick and pale. Whisking slowly, add the egg, flour, cinnamon, cloves and ground almonds, a little at a time. Gather the dough into a ball, wrap in cling film, and put it into the fridge for about an hour.

Preheat the oven to 180°C/350°F/Gas Mark 4. Lift the dough onto a lightly floured surface and roll out about three-quarters of the mix and lift onto a 20cm/8in loose bottomed flan tin, pressing it well into the edges. Spread the raspberries over the cake and sprinkle with a little sugar.

Gather all the remaining pieces of dough and roll out into a long enough oblong to be able to cut strips with which to make a lattice pattern over the raspberries.

Bake the cake in the oven for about 25 minutes or until it is pale golden brown.

Allow to cool before removing the cake from its tin.

MEDIVNYK / HONEY CAKE

UKRAINE

I was reading the paper recently when an amazing photograph caught my attention – a bride whose dress was made from cream puffs! The bridegroom was a professional baker, such was his enthusiasm for cakes that he baked 1,500 cream puffs, sticking them together with caramel on the outer fabric of his bride's dress. They were married in the Ukrainian city of Uzhhorod.

But here is a Ukrainian cake we can all bake and eat. Honey cakes are perfect fork cakes and this particular recipe is delicious.

3 large eggs	450g/1lb plain flour
150g/5oz sugar	1 level teaspoon baking powder
225g/8oz honey	1 level teaspoon baking soda
125ml/4fl oz sunflower oil	1 level teaspoon ground cinnamon
Juice and zest of 1/2 orange	2 level teaspoons ground ginger
2 tablespoons plain yogurt	

Preheat the oven to 160°C/325°F/Gas Mark 3.

Break the eggs into a mixing bowl and add the sugar, honey, oil, orange juice, zest and finally the yogurt. Using a hand mixer on a low speed, beat together until smooth. Add the flour, baking powder, baking soda, cinnamon and ginger, beat slowly until they form a creamy batter.

Pour or spoon the batter equally into two 900g/2lb loaf tins lined with greaseproof cases and place into the centre of the oven.

Bake for about 30-40 minutes or until well risen. Carefully open the oven door and press the top of the cakes, if firm the cakes are cooked, if not turn down the temperature of the oven to about 140°C/275°F/Gas Mark 1 and cook for a further 10 to 15 minutes or until the top feels firm when gently pressed.

Turn the cakes out onto a wire rack to cool.

TOMATO SOUP CAKE

CANADA

BBC broadcaster, Anna McNamee, sent me this recipe after we had recorded a radio series together on cakes. Born in Canada, Anna had often spent long snowy winter afternoons studying in a café, warming her hands on a cup of coffee. There was always a selection of two or three cakes of the day, one of which when you cut into it was a deep orange-red colour. It was delicious and turned out to be a 'tomato soup cake', which became her firm favourite. At first I was sceptical but since trying it for myself I have to agree with her, strange as it may seem it is good and certainly a talking point. If you find the recipe a little large, halve the ingredients and bake in a 18cm/7in cake tin for about an hour and ten minutes.

700g/1lb 8oz self-raising flour
1 1/2 teaspoons baking soda
2 teaspoons ground cinnamon
1/2 teaspoon allspice
1/2 teaspoon nutmeg
1/2 teaspoon ground cloves
250g/9oz softened butter
450g/1lb soft pale brown sugar
2 large eggs

295g tin condensed tomato soup
250g/9oz pecan nuts
175g/6oz chopped dates

Icing
225g/8oz soft cream cheese
225g/8oz softened unsalted butter
250g/9oz icing sugar, sifted
2 teaspoons vanilla extract

Preheat the oven to 180°C/350°F/Gas Mark 4. Sift together the self-raising flour, baking soda and spices and set it aside. In a large bowl cream the butter with the sugar until light and fluffy. Slowly add the eggs, beating until the mixture is glossy and smooth.

Make the tomato soup up to 450ml/16fl oz with the addition of cold water, whisking it until smooth, as it can be a little lumpy. Stir in the flour mixture and the soup alternately into the butter, sugar and eggs and when combined, fold in the pecan nuts and chopped dates.

Pour the mixture into a greased and lined 23cm/9in cake tin and place in the centre of the preheated oven, cooking for about 50-60 minutes or until the top feels firm to touch. Leave the cake to cool in the tin for about 20 minutes before turning out onto a cooling rack and leaving to become completely cold.

To prepare the icing, beat the cream cheese and butter together until fluffy. Add the sugar a little at a time, beating thoroughly before each addition; finally beat in the vanilla extract. Allow the icing to chill for about half an hour in the fridge (not longer or it becomes difficult to spread) before smoothing it over the top of the cake.

YOGURT TATLISI /YOGURT CAKE

TURKEY

Lemons and yogurt are very prominent ingredients in Turkish food, both savoury and sweet. Tatlisi is typical of so many sweet, sticky, aromatic Turkish cakes served while warm and accompanied by *kahvesi* (coffee). As most Turkish households also prepare yogurt freshly each day it is easy to see how it has become one of the most popular delicacies.

40g/1 1/2oz butter
200g/7oz caster sugar
5 eggs, separated
200g/7oz unsweetened yogurt
Finely grated rind of 2 lemons
250g/9oz self-raising flour
1/2 teaspoon bicarbonate soda

1/2 teaspoon baking powder

Syrup
150g/5oz white sugar
2 tablespoons water
Juice of 2 lemons

Preheat the oven to 180°C/350°F/Gas Mark 4.

In a large bowl cream together the butter and sugar before adding the egg yolks and yogurt a little at a time, stirring thoroughly. Fold in the finely grated lemon rind.

Stir in the flour, soda and baking powder. Whisk the egg whites until stiff before gently folding them into the cake mixture.

Pile into a greased and lined 18cm/7in cake tin and bake in the centre of the oven for 35-45 minutes until the cake springs back when pressed lightly in the centre.

Meanwhile put the sugar, water and lemon juice into a small saucepan and bring quickly to the boil, reducing the heat to allow the syrup to boil gently for five minutes. Set aside to cool a little.

When the cake has cooled for 30 minutes remove from the tin and place on a plate, spooning the syrup over the top, ensuring that it has been evenly covered.

Serve the cake slightly warm with cream or yogurt.

INDEPENDENCE DAY CAKE

USA

One thing that becomes clear as soon as you start to research American cakes is the important symbolism so many of them have within each ethnic group. Cakes such as the Amish Funnel Cake, Shaker White Mountain Cake, Indian Johnny Cake, African Creole Cake each tell their own story as does this Independence Day Cake which comes from the first American cookbook, written and published by Amelia Simmons in 1796. The book contained many errors since it would appear Amelia grew up in an orphanage and was probably illiterate but somehow I thought you would enjoy reading the recipe, even if it would be almost impossible to bake such quantities.

20lbs flour	2lbs citron peel
15lbs sugar	5lbs currants
10lbs butter	5lbs raisins
48 eggs	1 quart yeast
1 quart wine	
1 quart brandy	**Topping**
1oz nutmeg	Crushed loaf sugar
1oz cinnamon	Box cuttings
1oz cloves	Gold leaf
1oz mace	

Sadly, the temperature of the baking oven was not given, but I would imagine it would need to be cooked slowly. If you do try and succeed do let me know.

PAVLOVA

AUSTRALIA and NEW ZEALAND

Both Australia and New Zealand lay claim to the Pavlova. The recipe appears in a New Zealand recipe book in 1933 but by then Anna Pavlova, the famous Russian ballerina, after whom the cake is called, was dead so maybe it was first baked in Australia during the 1930s, in honour of her visit, as Australians claim. A tantalizing meringue cake, topped with whipped cream and fresh fruit, it often does double-duty as an elegant pudding. While it is easy to make it is however, important to follow the recipe carefully in order to bake a crisp meringue with a wonderful marshmallow-like centre.

Meringue base	**Filling**
3 egg whites	300ml/1/2 pint of double cream
175g/6oz caster sugar	Fresh fruit of your choice
1 teaspoon white vinegar	
1 teaspoon cornflour	

Preheat the oven 120°C/250°F/Gas Mark 1/2.

Line a baking tray with non-stick greaseproof paper and using a plate draw a circle of approximately 20cm/8in. Using an electric hand mixer, whisk the egg whites until stiff. Add half the sugar and whisk again, you will find the egg whites will become very stiff and stand in peaks. Fold in the remaining sugar using a metal spoon, stirring in a figure of eight, this ensures that all the air you have put in remains. Finally, add the vinegar and cornflour and spoon the mixture into a large piping bag. Start piping the meringue in circles from the centre of the paper working outwards until it is complete. Pipe your last circle on top of the outer ring to form a 'nest' for your cream and fruit. Place on the bottom shelf of the oven and check after one hour and then every 20 minutes until the outer meringue forms a pale 'crust', the centre should be cooked but very soft.

Carefully slide the Pavlova base off the greaseproof paper and allow to cool on a rack. When completely cold, transfer the meringue to a plate, don't worry if it cracks a little at this stage, you will be able to cover it with cream. Liberally pile on the freshly whipped cream and fruit of your choice and then sit back and admire your achievement.

SWEET DAMPER

AUSTRALIA

In Colonial days cooking conditions for the Australian settlers were very basic, and equipment virtually non-existent. Damper, enhanced by sugar, was perfectly acceptable as a very basic cake, the preparations being simple and baking taking place in the ashes of a hot fire, often outside. Any sweet ingredients which were available, honey, fruits or nuts, could be added. We will however, allow you to use an oven to bake your Damper and the recipe has been slightly updated by the use of self-raising flour, which gives a lighter texture.

450g/1lb self-raising flour	1 tablespoon honey
50g/2oz butter	300ml/1/2 pint milk
50g/2oz soft pale brown sugar	150ml/1/4 pint water
50g/2oz golden sultanas	

Preheat the oven to 180°C/350°F/Gas Mark 4.

Sift the flour into a large bowl and rub in the butter. Make a well in the centre of the mixture before adding the sugar, sultanas, honey, milk and water.

Stir the ingredients together with a pallet knife to form a dough. Lift it out onto a lightly floured surface and knead for 2 or 3 minutes.

Shape the dough into a round of about 15cm/6in in diameter and lift onto a greased baking tray. Cut a shallow cross onto the top of the Damper and bake in the centre of the preheated oven for about 25 minutes or until it is golden brown and sounds hollow when tapped on the bottom. Best served while warm.

REVANI / SEMOLINA CAKE

TURKEY

Revani appears to have several variations and I guess a Turkish baker would consider all of them to be typical examples of the recipe. The version I have chosen is simple, steeped in lemon syrup after baking and cut into squares before serving.

75g/3oz semolina	**Syrup**
115g/4oz plain flour	175g/6oz caster sugar
1 tablespoon baking powder	425ml/3/4 pint water
75g/3oz soft pale brown sugar	Juice of a lemon
1 tablespoon olive oil	
Zest of a lemon	
4 eggs	

Preheat the oven to 190°C/375°F/Gas Mark 5.

Weigh the semolina, flour and baking powder into a bowl and stir well.

Using an electric hand mixer, blend the sugar, olive oil, lemon zest and eggs together and pour them onto the semolina mixture. On slow speed blend them until completely mixed.

Pour the cake mixture into a greased and lined 20x20cm/8x8in square cake tin and bake in the centre of the oven for about 20-30 minutes. When cooked the cake will feel firm to touch, leave the cake in the tin to cool a little.

While the cake is baking, measure the syrup ingredients into a small saucepan and boil for 5 minutes.

While still in the tin, cut the Revani into evenly sized portions and gently pour over the lemon syrup, ensuring you cover the whole cake.

Remove the cake portions from the tin, when completely cold.

PENNSYLVANIAN DUTCH PUMPKIN CAKE

USA

I found it particularly intriguing when researching the cakes of the Amish communities in America to see the connection with their ancestors; many of their traditional recipes were brought with them from Holland and many still retain the Dutch origins in their names.

450g/1lb wholemeal plain flour	1/2 teaspoon ground cloves
2 teaspoons baking powder	275g/10oz softened butter
1 teaspoon baking soda	275g/10oz pale soft brown sugar
1 teaspoon ground ginger	5 eggs, lightly beaten
2 teaspoons ground cinnamon	275g/10oz cooked, mashed pumpkin
1/2 teaspoon ground nutmeg	115g/4oz sultanas

Preheat the oven to 160°C/325°F/Gas Mark 3.

In a large bowl, sift together the flour, baking powder, baking soda, ginger, cinnamon, nutmeg and cloves.

In a separate bowl cream together the butter and sugar until light and fluffy.

Add the eggs to the butter and sugar, alternating a little egg with a little of the spiced flour in order to prevent the cake mixture from curdling.

Finally stir in the mashed pumpkin and sultanas.

Spoon the cake mixture into a lined 20cm/8in cake tin and bake in the centre of the preheated oven for about 50 minutes or until the top of the cake feels firm, when gently pressed.

Leave to cool for a few minutes before turning out onto a wire cooling rack.

When the cake is cold, carefully peel away the greaseproof paper and place onto a serving plate. This is great with whipped cream.

KRANSEKAKE /WREATH CAKE

NORWAY

I truthfully did not know where to begin with this beautiful cake; everything I read told how difficult it was to bake, how you could make it with perfection one day, while on another it may be a total failure. Added to that, traditionally bitter almonds are used, which are poisonous if eaten before they have been baked when they lose their toxins. However, with a little research I found that ordinary ground almonds are perfectly acceptable, just making the cake a little paler.

But in spite of all that I could not leave the cake out of the book; no Norwegian home would be without one at any family celebration particularly Christmas, and decorated to fit the occasion so a wedding cake would have pretty fresh flowers on the top and a Christmas cake would have tiny red bows and Norwegian flags.

Meringue paste	**Icing**
450g/1lb ground almonds	225g/8oz icing sugar
450g/1lb icing sugar, sifted	1 egg white
3 egg whites	

Firstly draw onto the baking paper a series of circles beginning with the 25cm/10in reducing by 1cm/1/2in each time and finishing with a 5cm/2in circle. Place as many as will comfortably fit onto baking trays, bearing in mind that you may need to devise a baking 'rota' if you cannot fit all the baking paper circles onto your trays or all the trays into the oven at once.

Preheat the oven to 180°C/350°F/Gas Mark 4. Using a food processor, mix the ground almonds and icing sugar briefly at high speed. Add the egg whites, mixing at a lower speed until a thick paste is formed. Spoon the paste into a large piping bag with a plain 2.5cm/1in nozzle, and carefully pipe the mixture around the circle you have drawn.

Cook the meringue cakes in the preheated oven for about 20 minutes or a little longer until golden but still soft in the middle. Very carefully slide each cake ring from the baking sheets onto wire cooling racks and leave to become cold.

Mix the icing sugar with egg white, using enough to form a fairly thick consistency.

When the rings are completely cold, they are stacked into a pyramid, held together by squiggles of white icing. So place the largest onto a platter and squiggle on some icing using a piping bag and small nozzle, repeating the process until the cake is finished and you will be able to stand back and admire your wonderful pyramid of meringue rings. The only thing left to do is to decorate and wait for the praise you will undoubtedly receive.

TORTA DE TRES LECHES / THREE MILK CAKE

VENEZUELA

When I first read about this cake, I was puzzled as to how you could bake a cake with such large quantities of milk unless it was a batter. But I quickly realised that you did not in fact incorporate the various milks into the cake mixture, after cooking the cake is pierced and the combined 3 milks are used to steep the cake.

115g/4oz softened butter
225g/8oz caster sugar
225g/8oz self-raising flour
6 eggs, lightly beaten
1 teaspoon vanilla extract

2 tablespoons brandy
300ml/1/2 pint milk
175g/6oz condensed milk
175g/6oz evaporated milk

Topping
300ml/1/2 pint double cream
4 tablespoons icing sugar

Preheat the oven to 180°C/350°F/Gas Mark 4.

In a large bowl cream the butter and sugar together until light and fluffy. Add the flour and eggs a little at a time, using a mixer on low speed. Finally, add the vanilla extract.

Spoon the cake mixture into a well greased 23x30cm/9x12in square baking tin and cook in the preheated oven for about 25-30 minutes or until a skewer inserted into the centre of the cake comes out cleanly.

Leave the cake to become cold, before piercing it evenly over the surface.

Meanwhile mix the brandy and three milks together and spoon over the cake. Refrigerate overnight.

Before serving the cake, whisk the double cream and icing sugar together and spread over the top of the cake.

Keep the cake refrigerated until you are ready to serve it.

CARROT CAKE

USA

Originating in America, carrot cake is now just as popular all over the world. Traditionally decorated with a cream cheese icing, it is very easy to make, very moist and wonderful to eat either with coffee mid morning or a cup of tea in the afternoon.

225g/8oz soft pale brown sugar
3 eggs, lightly beaten
150ml/¼ pint vegetable oil
Zest and juice of an orange
225g/8oz self-raising flour
1 teaspoon cinnamon
275g/10oz finely grated carrot

50g/2oz chopped pecan nuts (optional)

Topping
225g/8oz cream cheese
115g/4oz icing sugar
1 tablespoon fresh orange juice

Preheat the oven to 180°C/350°F/Gas Mark 4.

Measure the sugar, eggs, oil, orange zest and juice into a large bowl and using a hand held electric mixer, beat together on a low speed.

Mix in the flour and cinnamon a little at a time to ensure it is lump free.

Finally stir in the carrots and pecan nuts and spoon the cake mixture into a greased and lined 20cm/8in cake tin. Bake in the centre of the preheated oven for about 1½ hours or a little longer if necessary, until a skewer inserted into the centre comes out cleanly.

Allow the cake to cool a little before turning out onto a cake rack. Remove the greaseproof paper and allow the cake to become completely cold.

Finally cream together the topping and spread over the cake, leaving it to set before eating.

This cake is best stored in an airtight container in the refrigerator.

JEWISH HONEY CAKE

ISRAEL

Rosh Hashanah, the Jewish New Year celebration, is the occasion when Honey Cake is eaten to symbolise a sweet and happy New Year.

Baked in a ring cake tin, the cake is wonderfully spicy and may be drizzled with a little warm honey after it has been turned out onto a serving plate. This cake is very difficult to resist when taken from the oven, as it is very aromatic and tastes great eaten while still warm.

3 large eggs
225g/8oz liquid honey
225g/8oz soft pale brown sugar
150ml/1/4 pint vegetable oil
450g/1lb self rAising flour
1 level teaspoon ground cinnamon

1/2 level teaspoon ground ginger
1/2 level teaspoon ground cloves
1/2 level teaspoon ground nutmeg
1 grated apple
50g/2oz golden sultanas

Preheat the oven to 180°C/350°F/Gas Mark 4.

Mix the eggs and honey together in a large bowl. Stir in the sugar, oil, flour and spices. Using a hand held electric mixer, beat them together until they are completely incorporated and lump free. Stir in the apple and sultanas and spoon the cake mixture into an oiled and lightly floured 20cm/8in ring cake tin.

Bake in the centre of the preheated oven for about 1 hour or until the cake is firm to touch and a skewer inserted into the cake comes out cleanly.

Allow the cake to rest for 10 minutes before carefully turning it out onto a rack to cool.

If liked drizzle a little warmed honey over the cooling cake.

HALVAS FOURNO / SEMOLINA CAKE

GREECE

Greek cakes are often baked in shallow oblong or square tins, topped with hot syrup and cut into diamonds or squares when cool. Semolina Cake is no exception, simple to make and simple to eat it is wonderfully aromatic and seems perfect served with a tiny cup of strong Greek coffee, which balances the sweet syrupy taste of the cake.

125g/4oz butter
175g/6oz soft brown sugar
Zest of 2 lemons
3 large eggs
225g/8oz semolina
150g/5oz plain flour
3 teaspoons baking powder

250ml/9fl oz milk
Flaked almonds

Syrup
400g/14oz caster sugar
500ml/18fl oz water
Juice of 2 lemons

Preheat the oven to 180°C/350°F/Gas Mark 4.

Weigh all the ingredients except the flaked almonds into a large bowl and using a hand beater gently cream the mixture, slowly increasing the speed of the mixer to incorporate the cake mix until smooth and creamy.

Spoon into a well greased 18x28cm/7x11in square baking tin and smooth the top, sprinkling it lightly with the flaked almonds evenly across the top.

Bake in the hot oven for about 45 minutes until it feels firm when pressed with the fingertips.

Meanwhile in a small saucepan bring the syrup ingredients to the boil then simmer for 5 minutes or until it starts to thicken.

Set the syrup aside to cool slightly before pouring gently and evenly over the top of the baked cake.

Leave the cake to cool completely before cutting it into squares for serving.

VIENNESE CURD CHEESECAKE

AUSTRIA

This lovely cheesecake is from a recipe given to me many, many years ago and which I have prepared and served on countless occasions. It is not quick to make, but it is perfectly straightforward and well worth the effort. Serve it with fresh fruit.

175g/6oz digestive biscuits	115g/4oz caster sugar
50g/2oz butter, melted	10g/1/2 oz gelatine, dissolved
25g/1oz caster sugar	3 drops pure vanilla extract
	3 egg whites
350g/12oz curd cheese	225g/8oz double cream, lightly whipped

Place a 18cm/7in buttered flan ring onto a serving plate, ensuring that the ring can sit flat.

Crush the digestive biscuits and stir in the melted butter and caster sugar. Spoon half of the biscuit mixture into the flan ring, pressing it down with the back of a spoon.

In a bowl, cream the curd cheese and sugar together and beat the dissolved gelatine into the mixture, add the vanilla extract and stir to ensure the mixture is well combined.

Whisk the egg whites until stiff and gently fold into the cake mix with a metal spoon before stirring in the lightly whipped cream.

Pile the cheesecake mixture into the flan ring, smoothing the top. Finally sprinklE the remaining biscuit crumbs on top of the cake mix, being sure to spread them evenly and put the cake in the refrigerator to set, it will take two or three hours.

BAKED LEMON CHEESECAKE

USA

Extremely popular in America, cheesecakes are also widely eaten throughout eastern Europe. This baked cheesecake recipe is easy to prepare and can be eaten as either a cake or a pudding.

115g/4oz digestive biscuits, crushed
900g/2lb cream cheese
225g/8oz caster sugar
Zest of 2 lemons

4 tablespoons lemon juice
1 teaspoon vanilla extract
4 large eggs
50g/2oz golden sultanas

Preheat the oven to 160°C/325°F/Gas Mark 3.

Sprinkle the crushed digestive biscuit evenly over the base of a well greased 23cm/9in spring form cake tin, pressing them down with the back of a spoon.

Place the cake tin onto the centre of a large circle of foil and pull the surplus up around the sides of the cake tin. With an electric hand mixer cream the cheese until smooth, add the sugar and beat again. Slowly add the zest and lemon juice, beating at a low speed. Add the vanilla.

Add the eggs to the cake mixture, a little at a time beating gently and stir in the golden sultanas.

Spoon the cheesecake mix into the cake tin and smooth the top.

Place the cheesecake in its tin, inside a larger round cake tin or roasting tin and fill the outer tin with water, ensuring that it reaches half way up the side of the cheesecake tin.

Bake in the centre of the preheated oven for about 1 1/2-1 3/4 hours or until the cake is golden brown and feels firm when pressed very gently, in the centre.

Remove the cake tin from the outer tin and allow the cheesecake to cool. Refrigerate overnight to allow the cake to become completely cold. Run a knife around the inner edge of the cake tin before removing the outer edge of the spring form tin and sliding the cake from the base.

RICOTTA CHEESECAKE

ITALY

A classic Italian cheesecake. Traditionally baked with brandy, candied peel, lemon and ground almonds, and using ricotta cheese, which is wonderfully creamy and readily available from most delicatessens or supermarkets.

450g/1lb ricotta cheese	75g/3oz ground almonds
4 medium eggs, separated	50g/2oz chopped candied peel
75g/3oz caster sugar	Zest of 2 lemons
50ml/2fl oz brandy	

Preheat the oven to 180°C/350°F/Gas Mark 4.

Beat the ricotta cheese, egg yolks and sugar together until creamy. Stir in the brandy, ground almonds, candied peel and lemon zest.

In a clean bowl whisk the egg whites until stiff and using a metal tablespoon, fold them into the cheesecake mixture.

Spoon the mix into a 20cm/8in greased and lightly floured spring release cake tin and bake on the lowest shelf in the preheated oven.

Check the cake after 40 minutes or until it is golden brown. The cake should feel firm to touch.

Remove the cake from the oven and allow it to become completely cold before removing it from its tin.

LADY BALTIMORE CAKE

USA

A delectable cake with an alcoholic fruit icing, the recipe for which first appeared in 1906 in a novel entitled *Lady Baltimore* by Owen Wister who is perhaps best known as the author of Wild West stories such as *The Virginian*. However, the recipe for the Lady Baltimore cake has brought him fame amongst cake enthusiasts all over the world, cowboys or not.

You may wonder what happens to all the egg yolks left from this cake, but don't worry I am assured that there is a Lord Baltimore Cake which uses only egg yolks.

Fruit filling
50g/2oz pecan nuts, chopped
50g/2oz sultanas
50g/2oz dates, chopped
3 tablespoons Cognac or sherry

125g/4oz softened butter
250g/8oz caster sugar
1/2 teaspoon vanilla extract

7 large egg whites
150g/5oz plain flour
1 teaspoon baking powder

Filling and icing
175g/6oz icing sugar
2 egg whites
4 tablespoons water
1/4 teaspoon cream of tartar

Steep the fruit and nuts in your chosen alcohol for at least 2 hours, stirring occasionally.

Preheat the oven to 160°C/325°F/Gas Mark 3. Cream the butter and sugar until light and fluffy, adding the vanilla extract.

In a clean bowl whisk the egg whites until they are very stiff and stand in peaks. Sift the flour and baking powder before adding a little at a time to the egg whites, stirring with a large metal spoon and being careful not to knock out all the air in the egg whites.

Combine the two mixtures, still using the large metal spoon, before dividing equally between two greased and lightly floured 20cm/8in sandwich cake tins and smoothing the tops. Place in the centre of the oven and bake for approximately 35 minutes or until a skewer inserted into the middle of the cakes comes out cleanly.

Leave the cakes for 5 minutes to cool a little before turning out onto a wire rack and leave until cold.

Sift the icing sugar into a bowl together with the egg whites, water and cream of tartar. Place the bowl over a pan of hot water and whisk with an electric hand mixer until the frosting is thick and stands in peaks. Stir in the chopped fruits and nuts before spreading about half of the frosting between the two layers of the cake, generously piling the remaining frosting onto the top and sides of the cake.

LAYER CAKES

It is almost impossible for a layer cake to appear boring and a lot of the layer cakes are actually rather famous, such as Dobos Torte; baked from five or six layers of sponge cake, it is unusual in that the cakes are not baked in tins, but spread in circles on greaseproof paper and when cooked they are layered with a rich chocolate filling and topped with crushed caramel.

One truly spectacular cake is the Indonesian Lapis Legit Cake which is baked by building up layer upon layer of a batter mixture, each new layer being baked on top of the previous one, building up to about 25 layers of cake. As you can imagine, this cake is pretty spectacular when sliced and served in a way which allows the numerous layers to be the feature.

Another cake baked in a very similar manner to the Lapis Legit Cake, is the Indian Babinca Cake, where the batter is made with coconut milk and layered with ghee.

Finally a recipe I must just mention is the Baumkuchen or Tree Cake, which is baked on a spit, practically impossible to recreate at home. A lot of argument has always raged about which region in Germany can lay claim to this complicated and very time consuming cake. This would be quite enough if it wasn't for the fact that another country also lays claim to it – Switzerland. The recipe ingredients make a gallon of batter. Even reading about the cake defeats me, as rather than horizontal layers, the layers (a minimum of 15 layers and up to 25, depending on the skill of the baker) are added to a rotating spit, producing a cake which has rings as you would see them if you sliced through the trunk of a tree, hence the name. But I do know that it would take several hours to put together, so I have stopped at reading and writing about it and have not given a recipe!

ZUGER KIRSCH TORTE

SWITZERLAND

Let me admit to my attachment to this cake, richly flavoured with the cherry liqueur, Kirsch. My view of Switzerland is maybe rather rose tinted, or should I say cherry tinted, but my memory of eating warm rolls for breakfast with the most incredible cherry jam, half way up a mountain, is indelible. Although this famous cake will take a time to prepare, it is well worth the effort.

Japonais layers
4 egg whites
150g/5oz icing sugar
115g/4oz ground almonds
1¹/2 tablespoons cornflour

Sponge layer
115g/4oz butter
115g/4oz caster sugar
115g/4oz self-raising flour
2 large eggs

Filling
150g/5oz softened butter
150g/5oz icing sugar
4-5 tablespoons Kirsch liqueur

Topping
A handful of flaked almonds
Icing sugar for dusting cake

Preheat the oven to 180°C/350°F/Gas Mark 4. Draw a 20cm/8in circle on each of 2 sheets of baking paper placing them on 2 baking trays. Using a hand held electric mixer, whisk the egg whites until stiff. Whisk in the icing sugar, until the mixture stands in peaks. Gently fold in the ground almonds and the cornflour. Spread half the Japonais mixture onto the two baking tray circles, smoothing them evenly and bake in the centre of the oven for about 15 minutes until they feel crisp to touch. Remove them from the oven, but leave them to become completely cold before removing the baking paper.

Meanwhile, measure all the sponge layer ingredients into a bowl and using the hand held mixer, whisk them together until pale and creamy. Spoon the cake mix into a greased and lined 20cm/8in sponge tin with a loose bottom and put into the centre of the oven for about 25 minutes until pale golden and springy when gently pressed in the centre. Leave to cool a little before turning out onto a wire rack and leave to become cold.

To make the filling, cream the butter and icing sugar together, slowly adding the Kirsch liqueur.

Putting the torte together is really simple. Place one of the Japonais cakes onto a serving plate and gently spread over a third of the filling, smoothing and topping with the sponge cake. If liked you can sprinkle a little liqueur over the sponge, before using another third of the filling to coat the top of the cake. Finally place the second Japonais cake on top and using the last of the filling, spread it over the top of the cake before sprinkling with some more flaked almonds and a dusting of icing sugar. Allow the filling to 'set' before serving.

LAPIS LEGIT / MULTI-LAYERED BUTTER CAKE

INDONESIA

Makes about 25 slices

Some of the cakes I have read about and studied in depth do not appear to be cakes in any normal sense. Sometimes it is quite simply the ingredients used, or maybe a cake will appear too complicated. The Lapis Legit from Indonesia is one such cake, but while thinking how I could make it simpler to bake, it occurred to me that I was committing a cardinal sin if I did not give the readers the correct recipe. This cake can be found at any celebration throughout the whole of the Indonesian archipelago and when cut shows the infinite number of layers of buttered cake, built up to 20cm/8in deep during baking.

30 egg yolks	I teaspoon vanilla extract
350g/12oz caster sugar	
115g/4oz self-raising flour	225g/8oz melted butter
675g/11/2lb butter, melted	Icing sugar for dusting top
4 level tablespoons condensed milk	

Preheat the oven to 180°C/350°F/Gas Mark 4.

Using a hand held mixer beat the egg yolks and caster sugar until pale, thick and creamy.

Sift the flour into the mixture and pour in the melted butter, condensed milk and vanilla extract, whisking gently until the batter is smooth.

Grease a square 20x20cm/8x8in cake tin (20cm/8in deep) with butter and line the base with greaseproof paper. Spoon about 5 tablespoons of the batter into the bottom of the tin, smoothing into the corners. Bake in the oven for about 5 minutes until golden brown. Remove from the oven and brush a generous amount of the melted butter over the top of the cake. Pour on some more batter and bake again until golden brown.

Repeat this process until the batter is completely used up, then remove the cake and allow it to become completely cold before running a sharp knife carefully around the outer edge and turning the cake onto a flat surface. Dust the top with a little icing sugar and cut the Lapis Legit into slices, working in the direction which will show the many slices of buttered cake.

BIBINCA

GOA, INDIA

The Portuguese ruled Goa for over 400 years and their influence can be seen everywhere and has left its mark on the cooking of the region. The cuisine is distinct because the ingredients are diverse but one of the key elements is the use of large quantities of coconut milk, such as in the Bibinca cake. It is a layered batter cake, not difficult to make but it is time consuming and does need care. Coconut milk and ghee are available from Indian supermarkets.

900g/2lb caster sugar
600ml/1 pint coconut milk
18 egg yolks

50g/2oz rice flour
2 teaspoons ground cardamom
225g/8oz ghee

Preheat the oven to 200°C/400°F/Gas Mark 6.

In a large bowl, stir the caster sugar and coconut milk together until dissolved.

Using a whisk beat the egg yolks until thick and creamy. Slowly pour on the coconut milk and continue to whisk, ensuring the ingredients are well mixed.

Whisk in the rice flour and cardamom.

Put a tablespoon of ghee into a 20cm/7in round cake tin and put into the oven, heat until smoking. Remove from the oven and carefully pour enough batter to cover the bottom of the cake tin. Put the cake back into the oven to cook, checking regularly. When cooked, remove from the oven and spoon over a little more ghee and some more batter, return to the oven. Repeat the process until you have used all the batter.

When the final layer has been baked, remove from the oven and turn the cake upside down onto a serving plate.

The Bibinca is then sliced with a sharp knife, showing the layers.

DOBOS TORTE

HUNGARY

József Dobos, a 19th century pastry chef, was the creator of this famous Hungarian cake. Quite unlike other sponges, the layers are not cooked in tins but spread into 5 or 6 evenly sized circles on greaseproof lined baking trays before baking. Cool before layering with a very rich chocolate filling and topped with crushed caramel. While the cake may seem complicated, it really isn't, all that's required is a little patience and believe me the result is well worth the effort.

6 eggs, separated
150g/5oz icing sugar
1/2 teaspoon vanilla extract
130g/41/2oz plain flour

Filling
175g/6oz unsalted butter
130g/41/2oz icing sugar

1/2 teaspoon vanilla extract
100g/3oz plain chocolate
1 egg

Topping
150g/5oz granulated sugar
3 tablespoons water
10g/1/2oz unsalted butter, melted

Preheat the oven to 220°C/425°F/Gas 7. Place the egg yolks and half the icing sugar into a bowl and whisk until light, creamy and increased in volume, stir in the vanilla extract. In a separate bowl whisk the egg whites until stiff and add the remaining icing sugar, whisking lightly until well incorporated. Fold the egg whites and flour lightly into the yolks a little at a time, using a large metal spoon.

Draw five 23cm/9in circles onto sheets of greaseproof paper and use greaseproof to line your baking trays, so you have five circles. Spoon the mixture evenly onto the circles and bake for 10 or 15 minutes. Remove from the oven, sliding the greaseproof sheets onto cooling racks and setting aside.

Meanwhile cream the butter and icing sugar together with the vanilla extract. Melt the chocolate over a saucepan of simmering water and when cooled stir into the butter and sugar together with the egg, beating until smooth and shiny.

Place one of the sponge circles onto a serving plate and layer with a little of the chocolate filling smoothing it well to the edges. Repeat until the sponge circles are stacked and finish with a layer of chocolate cream filling.

Finally make the caramel topping by placing the sugar and water into a small pan and bringing gently to the boil. Add the butter before cooking until the liquid becomes a light golden brown. Pour onto a greased baking sheet setting aside until cold, when it should be broken into tiny pieces and sprinkled onto the top of the cake.

PALACSINTA CAKE

HUNGARY

One of Hungary's most famous bakeries is the Gerbeaud in Budapest. Such is the reputation of this café-confectioners, that it really is the place to 'be seen'. Customers can watch the world go by while drinking coffee, chocolate or liqueurs, which are invariably accompanied by one of their truly wonderful cakes or pastries. The shop, opened by Henrik Kugler in 1858, has become famous for its many sweet delicacies including pancakes, often stacked into a gateau and filled with almonds or walnuts called the Palacsinta Cake.

6 eggs, separated	**Filling**
50g/2oz caster sugar	2 eggs, separated
175ml/6fl oz milk	50g/2oz icing sugar
50g/2oz self-raising flour	50g/2oz ground walnuts
25g/1oz butter, melted	50g/2oz ground almonds
	Zest of an orange
	6 tablespoons sour cream

Preheat the oven to 200°C/400°F/Gas Mark 6. Whisk together the egg yolks and sugar in a bowl, until thick and creamy. Add the milk, flour and butter a little at a time, to form a smooth batter. Whisk the eggs whites until stiff and using a large metal spoon fold them gently into the batter. Lightly grease a 20cm/8in frying pan and using a little batter at a time cook 4-5 pancakes. Stack them onto a plate and cover with a clean cloth while you prepare the filling.

Whisk the egg yolks with the icing sugar until they are thick and creamy. Fold in the ground walnuts and almonds together with the orange zest. Finally whisk the egg whites until thick and fold them gently into the filling.

Layer the pancakes and the filling into a greased 20cm/8in spring form cake tin, finishing with a pancake. Spread the sour cream carefully over the top and put the gateau into the preheated oven and bake for about 20 minutes or until the cake is golden brown.

Leave the cake to cool a little before removing from the tin and carefully lifting it onto a serving plate.

Dust with a little icing sugar and serve cut into wedges.

BATTER CAKES

Of all the sections in this book, none range so clearly from the practically impossible to the very easy, as batter cakes.

Spettekaka (Spit Cake) of Sweden is too difficult to bake in the average kitchen. It is a meringue-like cake, created by drizzling the batter of about 70 beaten eggs, sugar and a bit of potato flour slowly over a cone-shaped spit rotating over a slow fire, which forms many lacy layers. It is a huge cake and I have not included a recipe as so few people have the necessary rotating spits to bake the cake or indeed the ability or equipment to beat 70 egg whites until very stiff, but it is certainly one to look out for if you visit Sweden.

In contrast buckwheat pancakes are simple and quick to bake and it is easy to see how they were part of a staple diet in parts of America, when maybe the only place to cook was on an open fire. How much they must have been enjoyed when living in a wagon or an isolated cabin on a prairie, where it was difficult to cook anything other than the very simplest cake.

Japanese cakes are really fascinating and not necessarily how the rest of the world would recognise a cake. Sweet Bean Gongs for example are two small pancakes sandwiched together with an adzuki bean paste.

Batter cakes go back a very long way, milk and flour are the two basic ingredients although eggs, if available, enriched many recipes. One of the reasons why batter cakes have been so popular for centuries is the ease with which the mixture could be prepared and cooked. They really are cakes in their simplest form. A griddle was among the most used utensils in America and drop scones one of the most commonly made batter cakes, with just the addition of baking powder they rise and are flipped over before drizzling with maple syrup.

WAFFLES

BELGIUM

Waffles seem to be so much to the fore in Belgium, that it is impossible not to see them as the Belgians' most important cakes.

While they can be bought ready made and are usually very good, they are simple and enjoyable to make at home and I have always cooked ours using a waffle iron on the Aga hot plate.

I do also have an electric waffle iron, which may be something to consider if you begin to find making them rather addictive. Wonderful served with fresh cream, ice cream, syrup or seasonal fruits.

225g/8oz plain flour	2 large eggs separated
3 teaspoons baking powder	300ml/1/2 pint milk
50g/2oz caster sugar	50g/2oz butter, melted

Sift the flour and baking powder into a bowl and stir in the sugar. Make a well in the centre and using an electric hand mixer, slowly whisk in the egg yolks, milk and melted butter. Continue whisking until the mixture is smooth and lump free.

In another small bowl, whisk the egg whites until stiff and using a metal tablespoon, fold them into the waffle mixture.

Spoon a little waffle batter into a well greased, hot waffle iron and cook briefly on both sides. Check the waffle after a minute or two and when it is golden on both sides it is cooked. They do cook quite quickly, so check their progress regularly. Eat while still hot.

AMISH FUNNEL CAKE

USA

My mother's visit to the Lancaster County Amish Community in Pennsylvania enhanced my interest in their baking and I discovered that The Amish, Mennonites and Brethren communities have preserved many traditional foods.

Harshly persecuted in Europe, many moved to the USA in the 18th century and villages were established, enabling them to live their chosen lifestyles. Lack of electricity can make life rather difficult but none the less interesting, and baking still takes place on ranges, not so unlike our Aga when I think about it. Although today some things have crept into the lifestyle, if only to make the storage of food a little safer and the preparation a little easier.

Home grown crops and home produced ingredients are still the norm for many Amish homes and their cakes while traditional, often take considerable skill to bake. Probably the most well known is the Funnel Cake, named after the funnel used to pour the mixture onto the iron skillet. Served with maple syrup, they are sensational and they are still pretty scrumptious when simply covered with sifted icing sugar before being eaten.

275g/10oz plain flour	2 large eggs, lightly beaten
1/2 teaspoon baking powder	350ml/12fl oz milk
2 tablespoons caster sugar	

Place an iron skillet on to the hot plate and pour on enough oil to give a light covering.

Sift the flour and baking powder into a large bowl and stir in the sugar. Using a whisk, slowly add the eggs and milk until a stiff batter is formed, ensuring that no lumps are allowed to form.

Pour the batter into a jug and using a funnel, pour the mixture onto the hot skillet, beginning in the centre and slowly working your way to the outer edge. Continue until the cake is about 20cm/7-8in in diameter. When the cake is lightly browned, turn gently using a spatula, allowing it to cook on the other side. Immediately slide onto a plate and either sprinkle with icing sugar or pour over some maple syrup.

NIAN GAO / NEW YEAR CAKE

CHINA

There are many traditions associated with Chinese New Year or Spring Festival. One important tradition takes place before the end of the old year. According to legend, one week before the festival begins, the Kitchen God returns to heaven to report on a family's behaviour in the previous year. A bad report by the Kitchen God means a family will suffer bad luck in the year to come. So to ensure a good report from the Kitchen God, the custom evolved of feeding him a sticky cake. According to different accounts this was either a bribe, or simply a means of ensuring the Kitchen God's mouth was too full of cake to pass on an unfavourable report.

Most Chinese cakes are steamed but in this recipe it is baked so the cake will remain very moist in the centre but there is no cause for alarm – that is exactly how it should be. You may find Mochiko, sweet rice flour rather difficult to buy in your local supermarket, but there should be little problem in obtaining a bag from a Chinese supermarket or even from an on-line store.

450g/1lb Mochiko rice flour	1 tablespoon baking soda
115g/4oz butter	
3 large eggs	**Filling**
600ml/1 pint milk	1 tin red adzuki beans
175g/6oz sugar	

Preheat the oven to 180°C/350°F/Gas Mark 4. Lightly butter and dust with rice flour a 25x25cm/10x10in cake tin.

Put all the ingredients, except the adzuki beans, into a food processor and mix until smooth, this will take 3 or 4 minutes.

Pour half of the mixture over the base of the cake tin, ensuring it is fairly even.

Process the adzuki beans until fairly smooth and spread them over the batter, pouring the remaining cake mix over the top.

Place into the centre of the preheated oven and bake for about 45 minutes until golden and springy to touch.

Allow to become cold before cutting into pieces to serve.

DORA YAKI / SWEET BEAN GONGS

JAPAN
Makes 8-10

Probably one of the most popular Japanese cakes, Dora Yaki ('Dora' means gong and and 'yaki' means baking or grilling in Japanese) are generally eaten as one of the courses of a meal. They are easy to prepare and very good to eat, and are simply little pancakes sandwiched together by the sweet adzuki bean paste. You may prefer to use fresh adzuki beans rather than tinned ready-cooked ones which is fine, but it is important to follow the method carefully.

Sweet bean paste	Pancakes
175g/6oz adzuki beans	3 large eggs
(tinned, ready-cooked or fresh, see methods below)	150g/5oz caster sugar
	200g/7oz plain flour
225g/8oz caster sugar	1/2 teaspoon baking powder
1 tablespoon honey	3 tablespoons water

If using tinned beans, empty the adzuki beans into a medium saucepan together with the liquid in the tin. Add the sugar and honey and bring to the boil, stirring constantly. Reduce the heat and cook until almost all the liquid evaporates. Remove from the heat and set aside to cool a little before mashing the bean mixture to a smooth paste.

If using fresh beans rinse them thoroughly before soaking them in water for 5-6 hours. Drain and place the beans into a pan, covering with clean water. Bring to the boil and drain. Return the beans to the saucepan, cover with water and simmer until soft. Drain and return to the saucepan, adding the sugar and honey. Cook over a low heat, stirring until the sugar and honey have melted. Remove from the heat and allow to cool a little before mashing thoroughly. Use the sweet bean paste as required.

To make the pancakes break the eggs into a bowl with the sugar. Whisk until light and pale before slowly adding the flour a little at a time and whisking to form a batter. Heat a little vegetable oil in a large frying pan until it just begins to smoke, before spooning in enough mixture to form a pancake (gong) approximately 10cm/4in in diameter. When bubbles begin to rise to the surface, after a couple of minutes, flip over to brown on the other side.

Place the cooked gongs onto a folded tea towel, covering them to keep them soft as they cool. Finally, spread a little bean paste between two of the pancakes, continuing until all the gongs have been used. Best eaten the same day.

JOHNNY CAKES

USA

A very simple cake made from ground corn, which becomes far from simple when you realize just how many variations there are both in name and cooking methods. Was the name Johnny Cake originally Journey Cake or a twist on the Shawnee Indian word jonakin? Sometimes the cake is called a Hoe Cake and I have without any doubt seen 20 different names, whereas the recipes are all virtually identical. However, some aspects of the history of these corn cakes are much less palatable. Served with black treacle they were often all Negro slaves would receive, with little variation, day after day as rations.

Still as popular today, when a friend Belinda sent me a recipe I was not at all surprised to read that she always bought double the amount of corn meal, so that she was ready to bake another batch as soon as the first one was eaten. Not a bad recommendation.

150g/5oz cornmeal	50g/2oz caster sugar
250ml/9fl oz milk	
1/2 teaspoon dried or fresh dill	150g/5oz plain flour
1 egg	3 teaspoons baking powder
50ml/2fl oz sunflower oil	1 teaspoon salt

Measure the first six ingredients into a mixing bowl, whisking to combine them before setting aside for 10 minutes.

Preheat the oven to 190°C/375°F/Gas Mark 5.

Then add the flour, baking powder and salt to the mixture and stir thoroughly, before spooning it into a greased 900g/2lb loaf tin. Bake the cake for approximately 40 minutes before checking, it should feel firm to touch and a skewer inserted into the middle will come out cleanly, if not return to the oven and check every 10 minutes until cooked.

BUCKWHEAT PANCAKES

USA

When my children were tiny they loved me to read them Laura Ingalls Wilder books. They are stories of the way lives were lived on the prairies in North America and while I didn't feel particularly keen to kill and skin a bear to eat, we did often cook buckwheat cakes on the griddle and it was fun for them to experience a little of the cooking of that part of the world.

Simple to cook with only three ingredients plus some maple syrup, the buckwheat flour is usually available either from your local delicatessen or one of the larger supermarkets.

225g/8oz buckwheat flour
300ml/1/2 pint whole milk
1 large egg

maple syrup, to serve

Measure the flour, milk and egg into a basin and using a hand mixer, mix on a low speed to form a smooth batter.

Heat a large griddle greased with butter until it begins to bubble and pour on several rounds of the batter, each about 10cm/4in in diameter. Bubbles will begin to rise to the surface of the cakes and as soon as they have light browned on the underside, carefully flip them over using a pallet knife and cook until browned.

Spread out a clean tea cloth and put each cake onto the centre, building a pile and cover them over to keep them warm and moist.

When they are eaten, drizzle a little maple syrup over the top. Absolutely delicious and you too can imagine that you are in the middle of the American prairies.

FRUIT AND NUT CAKES

Even though I specialise in baking fruit cakes, I found myself remarkably ignorant when I began to research their history. Here in Britain fruit cakes were not really baked until the 15th century when dried fruits were imported from the Mediterranean together with spices. Perhaps because of the rarity of dried fruits, fruit cakes were always seen as special and were baked for weddings, christenings, Christmas and funerals. It was not until the 17th and 18th centuries that fruit cakes, similar to those we bake today, began to be widely cooked and eaten. Fruit was then often steeped in alcohol which not only gives richness but it meant that the cakes would remain fresh when stored.

Probably one of the most elaborate fruit cakes is the Sri Lankan Christmas Cake, which contains the most wonderfully varied fruits and nuts and the decorative marzipan is made from ground cashew nuts, rather than the more usual ground almonds.

The Black Cake recipe from the Caribbean is truly outstanding; the dried fruits are soaked in lots of alcohol and left to mature for about two months before going into the cake mixture. The Jamaican Rum Cake is also very special, the dried fruits are put into a large jar with enough rum to cover the fruits, which will eventually, after several months, be used to bake their wonderfully aromatic fruit cake.

The nut cakes are again very different, often containing little or no flour. The French Walnut Cake and the two Chestnut Cakes are good examples and of course there is a wide range of cakes in which ground almonds take the place of flour – all absolutely delicious with a wonderfully moist texture.

CHESTNUT CAKE

ITALY

Chestnuts are grown throughout Tuscany, where they thrive, so it is only natural that this wonderfully moist and aromatic cake is connected with this area.

350g/12oz cooked chestnuts	Zest of a lemon
6 egg yolks	150g/5oz ground almonds
225g/8oz soft pale brown sugar	50g/2oz plain flour
225g/8oz softened butter	5 egg whites

Preheat the oven to 180°C/350°F/Gas Mark 4.

Purée the cooked chestnuts. In a separate bowl, using an electric hand mixer, whisk the egg yolks and sugar together until pale and fluffy. On a low speed add the butter, zest, ground almonds and flour, ensuring that they are fully combined.

Whisk the egg whites until stiff and using a metal tablespoon, fold them into the chestnut mixture.

Spoon the cake mix into a greased and lined 20cm/8in round loose bottomed cake tin and put into the centre of the preheated oven. Bake for about 1 hour or until the cake is springy to the touch. Allow the cake to cool for about 10 minutes before removing it from the tin and leaving to cool on a wire rack.

PANFORTE

ITALY

Traditionally baked for Christmas, the Panforte has become a speciality of Sienna. An elaborate blend of chopped crystallized exotic fruits (available from most health food stores) such as pineapple, apricot, apple, papaya, oranges, lemon and lime, to which are added blanched almonds, walnut halves and pecans. Bound together with flour, spices and sugar syrup the cake is not only delectable it is really very 'different'.

350g/12oz candied fruit	1 teaspoon mixed spice
175g/6oz nuts	200g/7oz caster sugar
50g/2oz plain flour	4 tablespoons water

Preheat the oven to 160°C/325°F/Gas Mark 3. Line the base of a 20cm/8in loose bottomed cake tin with rice paper.

Place your choice of fruit and nuts into a large bowl, mixing them thoroughly.

Sift over the flour and spice and mix thoroughly again. Place the sugar and water into a small saucepan and stir over a low heat until dissolved before bringing the syrup to boiling point and then using a sugar thermometer, boil until it reaches a temperature of 120°C/250°F.

Taking considerable care not to splash yourself, remove from the heat and pour over the fruit mixture, stirring thoroughly before spooning into the cake tin and pressing down firmly.

Finally, bake in the oven for 30-40 minutes, the mixture will bubble but this is quite normal. Remove from the oven and run a knife around the edges before leaving to become completely cold. Remove from the tin and sprinkle with icing sugar before serving.

TORT ORZECHOWY / HONEY CAKE

POLAND   *Cuts into 8-9 slices*

This traditional Polish cake is very sweet and particularly moist. Made with ground almonds or hazelnuts, breadcrumbs are used rather than flour giving the cake its soft texture. I really enjoy this cake slightly warm but it is nonetheless delicious served cold.

225g/8oz set honey
50g/2oz caster sugar
4 eggs, separated

115g/4oz ground almonds or hazelnuts
175g/6oz breadcrumbs

Preheat the oven to 180°C/350°F/Gas Mark 4.

Spoon approximately three-quarters of the honey into a medium saucepan and melt very gently over a low heat. Remove from the heat and add the sugar and egg yolks, whisking vigorously.

Weigh the ground almonds or hazelnuts and breadcrumbs placing them into a medium bowl before pouring in the honey mixture, vigorously stirring with a wooden spoon. Finally, whisk the egg whites until stiff and fold gently into the cake mix.

Grease a 20cm/8in ring cake tin and flour well. Spoon the cake mix evenly around the tin and bake for 30-40 minutes until golden and firm when pressed lightly.

Allow to cool slightly before inverting onto a serving plate and gently heating the remaining honey to drizzle over the finished cake.

SIMNEL CAKE

ENGLAND

This is the recipe I gave in my last book, *Cakes Regional and Traditional* and if you want to read the full and fascinating history of this cake I refer you there. Briefly it is a mid-Lent cake which was baked and taken home by servant girls when visiting their mothers on what has become known as Mothering Sunday; it later became our traditional Easter Cake so it had to have a place in this book.

175g/6oz softened butter
175g/6oz pale muscovado sugar
3 large eggs
225g/8oz plain flour
50g/2oz ground almonds
1 teaspoon mixed spice
85g/3oz flaked almonds
175g/6oz sultanas
115g/4oz currants

175g/6oz raisins
75g/3oz chopped glacé peel
2 tablespoons Amaretto

Topping
550g/1 1/2lb almond paste
(may be purchased ready made)
2 tablespoons apricot jam

Preheat the oven to 160°C/325°F/Gas Mark 3 and grease and line a 18cm/7in round cake tin.

Cream the butter and sugar until light and fluffy, lightly beat the eggs and together with the flour, ground almonds and spice add a little at a time, stirring thoroughly. Fold in the flaked almonds and the fruits beating gently with a wooden spoon until thoroughly mixed and adding the 2 tablespoons of Amaretto.

Divide the almond paste into half, and divide one of the halves in half again. Roll one of the smaller portions into a circle of approximately 18cm/7in round and place the remaining 2 balls of paste in a polythene bag. Spoon half of the cake mixture into the bottom of the prepared tin, smoothing it carefully. Place one of the circles of almond paste on top and then spoon the remaining cake mixture into the tin. Bake in the oven for 1 1/2 hours and then covering the cake with a sheet of brown paper, reduce the temperature to 140°C/275°F/Gas Mark 1, continue baking for further 1-1 1/2 hours or until the cake is well risen and feels firm to touch. Because of the layer of marzipan in the centre of the cake, it is difficult to insert a skewer to check that the cake is cooked, as it is liable to come out 'sticky'. However, it should be possible to make a sensible judgement when the cake looks golden brown and baked. Leave in the tin until completely cold.

The following day, remove from the tin, and carefully peel away the greaseproof paper. Lightly brush the surface of the cake with warmed apricot jam and apply the second circle of almond paste to the cake top. Roll the remaining almond paste into 11 equally sized balls and position them around the edge of the cake. You may then place the cake briefly under a warm grill until browned, or as I prefer, use one of the now readily available chef's blow torches to brown the top of the cake and the 11 Apostle Balls, as they are known. When the cake is finished place a small posy of spring flowers in the centre before serving.

DUNDEE CAKE

SCOTLAND

This cake may date from the 17th century, when bakers created a cake for Mary Queen of Scots, who is said to have disliked cherries hence true Dundee Cake should never contain them. However it is also said to have been devised by Keiller's marmalade factory in the 18th century, as a way of using up some of their surplus orange peel. It is a cake that has great sentimental value for me. It was the first cake I baked when I had progressed from licking the bowl and stirring the mixture, to actually baking a fruit cake.

150g/6oz softened butter
150g/6oz pale muscovado sugar
150g/6oz plain flour
1 teaspoon baking powder
1 teaspoon mixed spice (optional)
4 large eggs
50g/2oz ground almonds
150g/6oz sultanas

115g/4oz raisins
50g/2oz currants
50g/2oz chopped candied orange peel
Grated zest of one orange
1 tablespoon brandy or sherry (optional)

Topping
18-20 whole blanched almonds

Preheat the oven to 150°C/300°F/Gas Mark 2. Cream the butter and sugar together until light and fluffy.

Sift together the flour, baking powder and spice. Beat the eggs in a jug and add the eggs and flour mixture alternately to the creamed butter and sugar, mixing slowly.

Stir in the ground almonds, dried fruit, zest and peel, using a large metal spoon. Finally add the brandy or sherry, if using. The mixture will be a soft consistency.

Spoon the cake mix into a greased and lined 18 cm/7in round cake tin, smoothing the top and arrange the whole blanched almonds in neat circles.

Place onto the lower shelf of the oven and bake for about 2 hours. Turn the oven down to 140°C/275°F/Gas Mark 1 for a further hour or until the cake is firm to touch and a skewer inserted into the centre comes out cleanly. Leave to cool in the tin for one hour before carefully turning out onto a wire rack.

GATEAU GRENOBLOIS /WALNUT CAKE

FRANCE

'A woman, a dog and a walnut tree
The more you beat them – the better they be'

While impossible to agree with such a sentiment, it is a fact that walnut trees are beaten to bring the nuts down to earth before laying them out on open racks to dry. The walnuts from Grenoble, where this cake recipe originates, are said to be the very best available. Walnut cakes are exceptionally rich, moistened by dense syrup, so do not be put off by the use of dried bread instead of flour - it really works.

2 slices white bread	**Topping**
150g/5oz butter	125g/4oz caster sugar
125g/4oz caster sugar	4 tablespoons water
4 eggs, separated	
Grated rind of 1 orange	Walnuts to decorate
150g/5oz ground walnuts	

Place the bread on a baking tray and allow to dry completely in a low oven. When cold, crunch to fine breadcrumbs (I find whizzing in a processor is quick and easy).

Preheat the oven to 160°C/325°F/Gas Mark 3. Line a 20cm/8in round cake tin with greaseproof paper and set aside.

In a medium bowl cream the butter and sugar before adding the egg yolks a little at a time, beating well between each addition to avoid curdling. Gently stir in the breadcrumbs, orange rind and ground walnuts until thoroughly incorporated.

In a clean bowl, whisk the egg whites until stiff and glossy before folding gently into the cake mixture. Working quickly spoon the mixture into the prepared cake tin and place in the centre of the preheated oven for about an hour or until a skewer inserted into the middle comes out cleanly.

Set the tin aside and allow to cool before removing the cake carefully and placing on a serving plate. Meanwhile place the sugar and water in a medium saucepan and place over a low heat, only stirring very occasionally. When the sugar has dissolved, bring to the boil and being very careful not to burn yourself from any spattering syrup, boil until it becomes a golden brown caramel. Then pour immediately but gently, all over the cake and leave to become cold. Decorate the top with some walnut halves if liked. The cake will be moist with a layer of crisp caramel on top.

CHESTNUT CAKE

HUNGARY

Chestnut cakes had managed to avoid me until I came across two recipes on the same day. As there are considerable differences in the recipes I have included both a Hungarian and Italian version. The following recipe is a delicious, very moist cake. Don't worry if it sinks as it cools, that is absolutely as it should be.

450g/1lb chestnut purée
115g/4oz softened butter
6 tablespoons rum
225g/8oz plain chocolate, melted
6 eggs, separated
175g/6oz soft pale brown sugar

Topping
175g/6oz plain chocolate
300ml/1/2 pint double cream
2 tablespoons rum

Preheat the oven to 180°C/350°F/Gas Mark 4. Using an electric hand mixer, slowly whisk the chestnut pureé, butter, rum and melted chocolate together, until they form a soft, well combined mixture.

In a separate bowl, whisk the egg whites until stiff and then using a metal tablespoon, gently fold them into the chestnut cake mixture.

Pour the mixture into a greased and lined 20cm/8in round, loose bottomed cake tin and bake in the centre of the oven for about 1 hour or until a skewer inserted into the centre of the cake, comes out cleanly. It may take a little longer to cook, but if the cake starts to brown too quickly, cover the top with a sheet of brown paper to protect it.

When the cake is cooked, leave it to cool in its tin for 5-10 minutes before turning it out onto a cooling rack and leaving it to become completely cold.

For the topping, melt the chocolate in a small saucepan before adding the double cream and rum. Stir until the topping reaches boiling point and remove from the heat. Ensure that the ingredients are completely combined and then gently pour the topping over the cake, spreading it with a pallet knife.

Allow the glossy topping to set completely before transferring the cake to a serving dish.

CACEN DDU / BLACK CAKE

PATAGONIA

From the 1860s Welsh families emigrated to Patagonia in large numbers to work in the gold mines, with the firm purpose of keeping their traditions, culture, religion and to perform agricultural work.

The Black Cake was born out of their need for wedding and Christmas cakes, and using scarce raw materials, they developed a recipe which ever since has been recognized by the Welsh colony as a typical Patagonian dish.

275g/10oz butter
275g/10oz dark muscovado sugar
450g/1lb plain flour
1 teaspoon baking powder
1 teaspoon cinnamon
2 teaspoons mixed spice
4 large eggs, lightly beaten
125g/4oz ground almonds
3 tablespoons black rum
1 teaspoon almond extract

225g/8oz currants
225g/8oz raisins
225g/8oz sultanas
125g/4oz chopped mixed peel
125g/4oz flaked almonds

Coating
225g/8oz icing sugar
A little boiling water

Preheat the oven to 150°C/300°F/Gas Mark 2.

Cream the butter and sugar together in a large bowl, until light and fluffy. In a separate bowl, sift the flour, baking powder and spices together and then stir them with the beaten eggs into the creamed butter and sugar.

Stir in the ground almonds, the black rum and the almond extract ensuring that it is well mixed and finally stir in the remaining ingredients. Carefully spoon the mixture into a greased and lined 20cm/8in cake tin, levelling the top.

Place in the centre of the oven and bake for 3 1/2-4 hours or until the top is firm to touch and a skewer inserted into the centre comes out cleanly. Cover with a clean cloth and leave to cool in the tin overnight and when completely cold, remove from the tin and place on a wire rack, removing the greaseproof paper. In a small bowl, sift the icing sugar and add enough water to form a smooth coating consistency. Finally spoon the icing over the cake, allowing the mix to run down the sides, giving it its traditional icing finish.

RUM FRUIT CAKE

CARIBBEAN

This is quite simply the most wonderful rich fruit cake imaginable, but if you want to bake one, you will need to start several months ahead to give the ingredients time to mellow.

The fruits are steeped in alcohol and spices and the longer they have to absorb the flavours, with only the occasional stir, the more aromatic they will be. I have tackled the recipe in two sections, firstly the preparation of the fruits and secondly baking the cake. This cake is wonderful decorated with a variety of glacé fruits.

450g/1lb currants	50g/2oz natural glacé cherries
450g/1lb raisins	2 teaspoons mixed spice
250g/8oz sultanas	6 tablespoons rum
225g/8oz pitted prunes	6 tablespoons brandy
115g/4oz chopped mixed peel	300ml/1/2 pint sherry

Wash the fruits and drain thoroughly, patting the fruits almost dry with a clean tea towel. Put the fruits into a food processor and chop in brief spurts. You do not want to end up with a fruit 'mash' so they will only need to be processed for a minute or two, to help the fruit absorb the spices and alcohol. Spoon the fruits into a bowl, add the mixed spice and pour over the rum, brandy and sherry, stirring thoroughly. Cover the bowl with foil, tucking it carefully around the edges and put it into the fridge, stirring every couple of days. The fruits will quite happily sit in the fridge for 2 or 3 months but they do need a minimum of 3 weeks to absorb the flavours.

450g/1lb dark muscovado sugar	4 tablespoons black treacle
450g/1lb fresh softened butter	450g/1lb self-raising flour
9 eggs, lightly beaten	

Preheat the oven to 140°C/275°F/Gas Mark 1. Cream the butter and sugar with a hand held mixer until they are pale and fluffy. Using a wooden spoon beat in the eggs, treacle and flour a little at a time to ensure the mixture does not curdle. Finally add the fruits, stirring to ensure they are evenly distributed. The mixture should be of a dropping consistency.

Spoon the cake mixture into a 23cm/9in round cake tin lined with a double layer of greaseproof paper and smooth the top. Tie a double thickness of brown paper around the outside of the tin.

Bake in the centre of the oven for about 3 hours, until it feels firm to touch and a skewer inserted into the centre, comes out cleanly. All ovens are different and please don't worry if it takes longer; just check every quarter of an hour, as an overcooked cake will be dry.

When the cake is cooked, leave in its tin until completely cold. Lift out and leaving its greaseproof jacket in place, wrap with an outer layer of foil, making sure the foil does not touch the surface of the cake. Store in a cool place until required.

DATE AND ALMOND CAKES

EGYPT   *Makes 12*

It is interesting to read that the early Egyptians ground their fruit and grains by rubbing them between two flat stones. Not so very different to how our local miller, Nigel Moon, grinds the flour for our cakes, in his painstakingly rebuilt windmill.

One thing in particular makes these cakes very special; they are sandwiched between wafer papers, before cutting into pieces; there is no cooking involved, so it is easy to imagine such cakes being made back in the earliest of times.

225g/8oz dates	Edible wafer paper
50g/2oz blanched almonds	
Zest and juice of $1/2$ lemon	
50g/2oz soft pale brown sugar	

Stone the dates and chop finely. Grind the blanched almonds, using a nut mill if possible.

In a small bowl mix the dates, almonds, lemon and sugar together, to form a thick paste.

Lay a sheet of wafer paper onto a board and spread with the date mixture, about an inch thick. Put a second wafer sheet on top and trim the edges with a sharp knife. Place another board on top and press the cake mixture down firmly. Leave overnight before cutting into equal sized fingers of cake. Store in a cool place.

BIBIKKAN / COCONUT CAKE

SRI LANKA

There are many variations of the recipe for Bibikkan – one of the most popular cakes baked in Sri Lanka. However one common ingredient is jaggery, the unrefined syrup and sugar from the sap of the date palm. This dark brown raw palm sugar is sold in a block from which you scrape or grate the required amount for your recipe. It is possible to purchase this type of sugar from grocery shops specialising in Indian or Middle Eastern foods, but if not, substitute dark molasses sugar.

225g/8oz jaggery
375ml/13fl oz fresh coconut milk
225g/8oz grated fresh coconut
50g/2oz semolina
1/2 teaspoon baking powder
75g/3oz chopped dates
1/2 teaspoon ground fennel seeds
1/2 teaspoon ground cardamom

1/2 teaspoon ground cinnamon
100g/4oz chopped glacé melon
25g/1oz ginger preserve
25g/1oz glacé peel
115g/4oz chopped cashew nuts
50g/2oz sultanas
1 large egg, separated

Preheat the oven to 160°C/325°F/Gas Mark 3.

Grate the jaggery into a saucepan and add the fresh coconut milk, heating gently to dissolve the sugar before adding the fresh coconut and cooking for 3-4 minutes. Allow to cool.

Stir in the semolina, baking powder, chopped dates, all the spices, ginger preserve, glacé melon and peel, cashew nuts and the sultanas. Beat the egg yolk lightly and add to the cake mix.

Whisk the egg white until stiff and gently fold it into the mixture.

Finally, spoon the Bibikkan into an 18cm/7in cake tin lined with a double layer of greaseproof paper and lightly smooth the surface. Bake in the centre of the oven for approximately 1 1/2 hours or until the top is golden brown and a skewer inserted into the centre of the cake comes out cleanly.

Allow the cake to cool completely before carefully removing it from the tin onto a serving plate.

ALMOND CAKE

PORTUGAL

This delectable cake, baked with ground almonds instead of flour, is prepared in a quite different way to most cakes, the preparation, taking place in a saucepan. The cake mix is cooked gently before pouring into a prepared cake tin. The result is really delicious.

450g/1lb pale soft brown sugar
100ml/4fl oz water
225g/8oz ground almonds
5 egg yolks, lightly beaten
5 eggs, lightly beaten

1 teaspoon ground cinnamon
1/4 teaspoon ground cloves
1/4 teaspoon ground mace

Toasted flaked almonds

Preheat the oven to 180°C/350°F/Gas Mark 4.

Measure the sugar into a saucepan with the water and dissolve slowly over a medium heat.

Add the ground almonds and stir over a low heat for 4 or 5 minutes. Set aside to cool.

Whisk the egg yolks, whole eggs and spices together before adding to the almond mixture. Stir thoroughly before cooking over a low heat until the mixture thickens, about 5 or 6 minutes.

Spoon the cake mixture into a greased 20cm/8in spring release cake tin, sprinkled with a little sugar, smoothing the top. Cook in the centre of the preheated oven until set, about 20 minutes.

Allow the cake to cool completely before removing from the cake tin and decorating with a small quantity of toasted flaked almonds.

CHRISTMAS CAKE

SRI LANKA

You may find it strange that Sri Lanka has a Christmas cake but the Portuguese, Dutch and British influences on the country's food have provided great diversity. Their Christmas cakes are not usually iced, but decorated with marzipan made from ground cashew nuts, before cutting into pieces and wrapping in decorative Christmas paper.

115g/4oz chopped stem ginger
115g/4oz chopped mixed peel
225g/8oz raisins
225g/8oz sultanas
225g/8oz currants
225g/8oz chopped crystallized pineapple
225g/8oz chopped cashew nuts
115g/4oz chopped almonds
115g/8oz chopped bright red glacé cherries
115g/4oz chopped dark red glacé cherries
3 tablespoons brandy
3 tablespoons rose water
2 tablespoons honey
2 teaspoons vanilla extract
2 teaspoons ground cinnamon
1 teaspoon ground mace

1 teaspoon ground cardamom
1/2 teaspoon ground cloves
450g/1lb soft pale brown sugar
450g/1lb softened butter
225g/8oz semolina
12 large eggs, separated

Marzipan
225g/8oz cashew nuts
450g/1lb icing sugar
1 egg white
4 tablespoons brandy
1 teaspoon almond extract
1 tablespoon rose water
1 teaspoon vanilla extract

Measure the peel and fruits into a large bowl adding the nuts, brandy, rose water, honey, vanilla extract and spices mixing together with a large metal spoon. Cover and leave overnight to allow the flavours to combine.

Line two 20cm/8in square cake tins with greaseproof baking paper and preheat the oven to 150°C/300°F/Gas Mark 2.

Using a hand mixer, cream the sugar and softened butter until light and fluffy. On a slow speed add the semolina and egg yolks a little at a time to avoid curdling. Using a large metal spoon add the fruit mixture and stir until completely blended.

Measure half the egg whites into a bowl and whisk until they stand in peaks, then using a metal spoon, stir the whites gently into the cake mixture.

Divide the cakes equally between the two cake tins and bake until a skewer inserted in the centre comes out cleanly – about 1 hour 45 minutes. Leave the cakes to become cold in their tins, before wrapping in foil and setting aside for three or four days to mature. After the cakes have been left to mature, prepare the marzipan.

Put the cashew nuts into a food processor and on the highest speed grind to a paste. Add the icing sugar and other ingredients, processing at the lowest speed, until you can gather the marzipan into a ball. Dust the work surface lightly with icing sugar and roll out the paste, if it is too sticky, roll between two sheets of greaseproof paper. Cut the topping into two circles and position on top of the cakes. You may roll paste more thinly and cover both cakes fully.

CHRISTMAS CAKE

ENGLAND

The Christmas cake as we know it today probably comes from a porridge, the origins of which go back to the beginnings of Christianity. It was a dish eaten after a day's fasting, which people used to observe on Christmas Eve. Gradually, they began to put spices, dried fruits, and honey in the porridge to make it a special dish for Christmas. And later it became popular to add butter, replace the oatmeal with flour and add eggs. This became boiled plum cake and very much part of the festival of Twelfth Night; the traditional day when Christians celebrate the arrival of the Magi at Bethlehem and the time when people exchanged Christmas gifts. However by 1870, Twelfth Night was banned as a feast day and the confectioners who had made cakes lost revenue by the ban. So they began to bake fruit cakes and decorate them with snowy scenes, which they sold, not for the 5th January, but for December Christmas parties. And it was thus that we developed the Christmas cake.

225g/8oz each of currants, raisins and sultanas	225g/8oz plain flour
50g/2oz chopped glacé peel	1 heaped teaspoon ground mixed spice
50g/2oz glacé cherries, halved	50g/2oz ground almonds
4 tablespoons brandy	4 large eggs, lightly beaten
225g/8oz butter	Zest of one large lemon
225g/8oz dark muscovado sugar	1 tablespoon lemon juice
1 dessertspoon black treacle	50g/2oz flaked almonds

The night before you plan to bake the cake, wash the dried fruit, peel and cherries, draining thoroughly. There is no need to dry the fruit, simply place it in a bowl, add the brandy and stir well. Cover and set aside to steep overnight.

Preheat the oven to 140°C/275°F/Gas Mark 1. Place the butter and sugar in a large bowl creaming until light and fluffy and then beat in the black treacle. In a separate bowl, sift the flour and spice, stirring in the ground almonds. Add the eggs to the butter and sugar, a little at a time, adding a tablespoon of the flour if the mixture begins to curdle. Fold in the remaining flour, together with the lemon zest and juice. Finally, add the fruit and flaked almonds stirring gently but thoroughly. When the cake ingredients are thoroughly mixed together, spoon them into a 20cm/8in round cake tin, lined with greaseproof paper and place into the oven on a low shelf. After 2 hours lower the temperature to 120°C/250°F/Gas Mark 1/2 covering the top of the cake with brown paper and bake for a further 1 hour or until the top feels firm and a skewer inserted into the centre comes out cleanly. Do not worry if it takes a little longer.

When the cake is cooked, leave in its tin and cover with a clean cloth. Allow it to become completely cold – at least 24 hours. Remove from the tin and leaving it in its greaseproof wrapping, over wrap with a second clean sheet of greaseproof, finally wrapping it tightly in foil. The cake will remain in excellent condition for three or four months if stored in a cool, dry, place until required for decoration. Decorate as you like with marzipan and royal icing.

KARIDOPITA /WALNUT CAKE

GREECE

A really delicious cake which reminded me a little of the Gateau Grenoblois, both cakes are traditionally baked and eaten in the walnut growing areas of their country.

What makes the walnut cake so very distinctive is quite simply that the flour is replaced with ground walnuts and a small quantity of breadcrumbs, plus the added spices, alcohol and oranges and lemons all help to produce a wonderfully aromatic cake.

8 eggs, separated
175g/6oz caster sugar
450g/1lb ground walnuts
25g/1oz breadcrumbs
2 tablespoons lemon zest

2 tablespoons orange zest
50ml/2fl oz brandy
50ml/2fl oz orange juice
1 teaspoon ground cinnamon
2 teaspoons baking powder

Preheat the oven to 180°C/350°F/Gas Mark 4.

Cream the egg yolks with the caster sugar until pale and creamy. Add the ground walnuts, breadcrumbs, lemon and orange zest, brandy, orange juice, cinnamon and baking powder.

Stir thoroughly to ensure they are really well blended.

In a separate bowl, whisk the egg whites until stiff and using a metal tablespoon, fold them into the nut mixture.

Spoon the cake mixture into a greased 30x23cm/12x9in cake tin and smooth the top. Bake in the preheated oven for about 25-30 minutes or until the cake feels springy to touch.

Allow the cake to cool in its tin before turning out and cutting into evenly sized pieces.

GUINNESS CAKE

IRELAND

This robust, moist, dark fruit cake is absolutely mouth-watering, made with the traditional Irish Stout Guinness; it should be kept for at least a week before eating.

75g/3oz sultanas	115g/4oz butter
75g/3oz raisins	225g/8oz dark muscovado sugar
75g/3oz currants	3 large eggs
75g/3oz chopped mixed peel	350g/12oz self-raising flour
150ml/¼ pint Guinness	1 teaspoon mixed spice

In a medium bowl place all the dried fruit and peel, pour over the Guinness and stir. Leave overnight to steep.

Preheat the oven to 180°C/350°F/Gas Mark 4.

Cream the butter and sugar together until light and fluffy and then beat in the eggs one at a time. Fold in the flour and spice using a metal spoon and when thoroughly combined, add the fruits, stir well and spoon the mixture into a greased and lined 18cm/7in cake tin. Smooth the cake top and place the cake in the centre of the preheated oven, reducing the temperature to 140°C/275°F/Gas Mark 1 after 1 hour. Continue to bake for a further hour or until a skewer inserted into the top of the cake comes out cleanly.

If the cake begins to brown too quickly, place a sheet of brown paper over the top of the tin.

When the cake is baked, allow it to cool completely in its tin before turning out and wrapping in clean greaseproof and foil and storing for 6 or 7 days to mature.

RUM CAKE

JAMAICA

There are many recipes for Jamaican rum cakes, each one appearing more indulgent than the last, but without doubt they are all absolutely delicious. One recipe involves simmering the fruits in red wine and spices, easily imagined if you enjoy mulled wine, as I do. The burnt sugar in this recipe is available from Caribbean shops. You do need to soak the fruits about 4 weeks in advance of baking.

450g/1lb prunes	2 tablespoons black treacle
450g/1lb raisins	450g/1lb plain flour
450g/1lb currants	2 teaspoons baking powder
450g/1lb cherries	2 teaspoons baking soda
	1 teaspoon cinnamon
450g/1lb butter	1 teaspoon nutmeg
450g/1lb dark muscovado sugar	12 eggs
1 teaspoon vanilla extract	
2 teaspoons burnt sugar	Rum as required

Chop all the fruits into smallish pieces before spooning them into a large jar with a sealing lid and pouring on enough rum to cover the fruit completely. Screw on the lid and store in a cool dark place for a few weeks.

Preheat the oven to 140°C/275°F/Gas Mark 1. It is essential to use an electric hand mixer for the preparation of this cake because it will be easier to cope with the large quantities involved. Cream together the butter and sugar until they become light and fluffy. Stir in the vanilla extract, burnt sugar and black treacle.

Sift together the flour, baking powder, baking soda and spices, before slowly adding the eggs two at a time and a little flour mixture at a time, using the mixer on the lowest speed. Take care not to allow the cake mix to curdle. Finally, add the fruits, which by now will have absorbed most if not all of the rum, ensuring that the ingredients are evenly mixed.

Pour the mixture into a greased and lined 23cm/9in round cake tin, with brown paper tied around the outside. Bake the cake in the centre of the oven, checking occasionally to ensure it is not cooking too quickly. Once the cake feels firm to touch and a skewer inserted into the centre comes out clean, remove from the oven and immediately spoon over 6 tablespoons of rum before allowing the cake to cool completely.

Once cold remove the cake from its tin and cover with another layer of greaseproof and a tightly wrapped layer of foil. Every 3 or 4 days unwrap the cake and spoon over 2 tablespoonfuls of rum. Do this for about 2 weeks or until the cake just cannot absorb any more alcohol! Allow the cake to mature a little longer, or eat now if you cannot wait.

CHOCOLATE AND COFFEE CAKES

Mexico is and always has been at the very heart of chocolate production. The cacao tree grows in what are the absolutely perfect conditions of the humid, dense tropical forest and thus chocolate has for centuries been regarded as a 'Gift from the Gods' there.

Originally the cocoa beans were only used to produce a chocolate drink, often with the addition of spices. By the mid-19th century, the first chocolate bars were made and it is not hard to see how with the popularity of chocolate and cocoa powder, experimentation led to some of the chocolate cakes which are today so well known. Austria Sachertorte was and perhaps still is, one of the most famous. The Italians and Germans quickly followed suit, experimenting and producing some amazing cakes such as the Black Forest Gateau.

Perhaps not quite so dramatically the coffee bean also began to create an interest and coffee houses were set up, often in rivalry to the numerous chocolate houses where even ladies could go, being rather 'the place to be seen'. Coffee however took a long time to establish itself in Europe, although it had been well loved in the Middle East for centuries.

SACHERTORTE

AUSTRIA   *Serves 18*

A great many myths have grown up around the invention of the Sachertorte; the most credible being that the master baker Franz Sacher was asked to produce a special cake which would appeal to the chocolate loving Austrian gentry. At the time, he was employed by Prince Klemens von Metternich and was heard to complain that 'he' kept on at him all the time so in the end Franz "threw some ingredients together and that was that" never foreseeing how popular the cake would become. Many arguments raged over the 'original' recipe, which has resulted in lawsuits and even the use of apricot glaze, now such an integral part of the cake, has become questionable.

Today Sachertortes are baked all over the world, but most importantly the cake can still be consumed with a cup of coffee in its original home Vienna and remains Austria's most luxurious treat.

225g/8oz plain 70% chocolate	**Filling**
115g/4oz unsalted butter	225g/8oz sieved apricot jam
1 teaspoon vanilla extract	
10 eggs, separated	**Chocolate topping**
150g/5oz caster sugar	150g/5oz plain chocolate
115g/4oz plain flour	200ml/7fl oz double cream
	50g/2oz milk chocolate for decoration

Preheat the oven to 180°C/350°F/Gas Mark 4. Melt the chocolate in a bowl over a saucepan of lightly boiling water. Remove from the heat. Add the butter, vanilla extract and egg yolks once the chocolate has melted, stirring constantly.

Whisk the egg whites and sugar until stiff and add gently to the chocolate mixture, spooning in a little at a time to retain the air. Finally, fold in the flour very carefully. Immediately spoon the cake mixture into two greased and lined 23cm/9in cake tins and bake for about 25-30 minutes or until the top feels firm when lightly pressed in the centre.

Allow the cakes to cool a little before carefully turning them onto wire racks and leaving to become cold. It is best to place the cooling rack over the cakes before inverting the tins, helping to avoid breaking the fragile sponges. When cold, warm the apricot jam and sandwich together to the halves of the cake. Place back onto a wire rack to apply the chocolate icing.

Meanwhile place the chocolate and cream into a bowl over a saucepan of lightly boiling water, stirring occasionally. Remove when the chocolate has melted and allow to cool slightly. Immediately pour over the cake and smooth with a palette knife. When set, melt the milk chocolate, place into a small piping bag and drizzle patterns over the Sachertorte. If liked you can pipe the word Sachertorte onto the top of the cake.

CHOCOLATE CAKE

MEXICO

Mexican food clearly reflects its Aztec heritage in using a whole range of native plants; maize, chillies, tomatoes, avocados and beans of many kinds. But there was of course one crop which led to a complete revolution both in drinks and sweets and as an admitted addict, I am of course talking about chocolate. Oddly enough, in Mexico most of their chocolate consumption is in the form of drinks, often with ground spices added. It was other countries which quickly took to using chocolate to create confectionery, cakes and puddings. The one clear exception is Mexican Chocolate Cake, but it proved less than simple to track down one definitive recipe, each family appearing to have their favourite added ingredients, such as cinnamon or even in one recipe I found chillies, giving the cake an indisputable warmth.

The recipe I have chosen is really very good indeed, the ground almonds providing the moist texture, which always goes so well with chocolate cakes.

350g/12oz muscovado sugar
275g/10oz self-raising flour
125g/4oz ground almonds
1 teaspoon baking soda
1 teaspoon cinnamon
4 tablespoons cocoa powder
350g/12oz softened butter
2 tablespoons vegetable oil
6 large eggs, lightly beaten
1 teaspoon vanilla extract

Chocolate topping
225g/8oz butter
4 tablespoons cocoa powder
6 tablespoons water
450g/1lb icing sugar
1 teaspoon vanilla extract

Preheat the oven to 180°C/350°F/Gas Mark 4. Grease and line a 23cm/9in spring form cake tin.

Mix the sugar, flour, ground almonds, baking soda, cinnamon and cocoa together in a bowl and set aside. Melt the butter and vegetable oil in a small saucepan over a low heat and beat into the dry ingredients, together with the eggs and vanilla extract, having ensured that there are no lumps before finally spooning the cake mix into the prepared tin and placing it into the centre of the preheated oven. Cook for about 30 minutes or until the top feels springy when pressed lightly in the centre.

While the cake is cooking melt the butter, cocoa powder and water in a small saucepan over a low heat, stirring until the ingredients have formed a smooth mixture. Remove from the heat and pour into a bowl. Finally beat in the icing sugar until smooth. When the cake is cold spread the chocolate topping onto the cake before serving.

SCHWARZWALDER KIRSCHTORTE / BLACK FOREST GATEAU

GERMANY

Kirsch, the famous cherry liqueur from southern Germany, gives the Black Forest Gateau its characteristic intensity. Three layers of chocolate sponge are steeped in kirsch and sandwiched together with stoned black cherries, black cherry jam and whipped double cream. The top of the gateau is finished with extra whipped cream and sprinkled with chocolate curls or flakes and perhaps a spray of fresh cherries for decoration.

225g/8oz plain 70% chocolate	**Topping**
115g/4oz butter	60ml/4 tablespoons kirsch
3 large eggs, separated	600ml/1 pint double cream, whipped
115g/4oz dark muscovado sugar	1 jar black cherry jam
115g/4oz self-raising flour	450g/1lb Morello cherries, drained
50g/2oz ground almonds	Grated or flaked chocolate
	Small number of fresh cherries

Preheat the oven to 180°C/350°F/Gas Mark 4.

Place a heatproof bowl over a pan of simmering water. Break the chocolate into pieces and put into the bowl with the butter, stirring until melted before lifting from the heat and allowing to cool. In a separate bowl whisk the egg yolks and sugar until they thicken, gently mixing into the chocolate and butter mixture. Whisk the egg whites until stiff and using a large metal spoon, fold in the flour, ground almonds and egg whites until completely incorporated.

Spoon the cake mixture into three greased and lined 20cm/8in sandwich cake tins and place into the oven for about 25 minutes or until well risen and firm to touch. Gently turn the sponges out onto wire racks, peeling the greaseproof paper from the bottom and leave to become cold.

When the sponges are cold, sprinkle evenly with the kirsch, before sandwiching together with the jam and black Morello cherries, using a third of the cream between each layer. Finally spread the top of the cake with the cream and sprinkle with the grated or flaked chocolate, finishing with a small number of fresh cherries for decoration.

BLACK MAGIC CHOCOLATE CAKE

USA

A very moist dark cake, which generally makes its appearance on celebration days but when I first saw this recipe, I somehow felt a chocolate cake was unusually rich for an Amish recipe; however, when the ingredients are considered, they are all very simple and straightforward.

275g/10oz plain flour	2 large eggs
350g/12oz dark muscovado sugar	275ml/10fl oz black coffee
150g/5oz cocoa powder	250ml/8fl oz milk
2 teaspoons baking powder	125ml/4fl oz corn oil
1 teaspoon baking soda	

Preheat the oven to 180°C/350°F/Gas Mark 4.

Sift all the dry ingredients into a mixing bowl, before adding the eggs, coffee, milk and corn oil. Gently whisk with a hand held electric mixer until the batter is smooth and lump free. Pour the cake mix into a lined 18cm/7in round cake tin and bake in the centre of the oven for about 40 minutes, or until a skewer put into the centre of the cake comes out cleanly.

Allow the cake to cool in its tin before turning out onto a wire rack. Don't worry if the cake sinks a little in the centre, this is quite normal.

MISSISSIPPI MUD CAKE

USA

Supposedly named after the dark muddy soil of the Mississippi river, with its thick, dark, muddy waters, there is also a Mississippi Mud Pie.

300ml/ 1/2 pint strong coffee	225g/8oz soft pale brown sugar
50ml/2fl oz brandy	225g/8oz self-raising flour
175g/6oz dark 70% chocolate	2 tablespoons cocoa
225g/8oz butter	2 large eggs, lightly beaten

Preheat the oven to 140°C/275°F/Gas Mark 1.

Measure the coffee, brandy, chocolate and butter into a heatproof bowl and place over a pan of simmering water, stirring until they have completely melted. Remove the bowl from the saucepan and stir in the sugar until dissolved.

Using an electric hand mixer, blend in the flour and cocoa, finally adding the beaten eggs.

Pour the cake mixture into a well greased and floured 23cm/9in ring cake tin and bake in the centre of the oven for about 1 1/2 hours, but do check it after one hour, as ring cakes can cook quite quickly. When the top feels firm and a skewer inserted into the cake comes out cleanly, the cake is cooked.

Place the cooling rack over the top of the cake, turning it upside down and shaking gently until the cake drops from the tin.

Leave to become completely cold before moving onto a serving plate.

COFFEE CAKE

ENGLAND

Bottled Camp coffee is perfect for making coffee cakes. However if you cannot find it in your local shop, as it is increasingly hard to track down, then coffee granules dissolved in a little hot water will be fine.

225g/8oz butter
225g/8oz caster sugar
225g/8oz self-raising flour
4 large eggs, lightly beaten
50ml/2fl oz Camp coffee or dissolved granules

Filling
225g/8oz icing sugar
115g/4oz butter
2 teaspoons Camp coffee or dissolved granules

Decoration
7-8 walnut halves

Preheat the oven to 180°C/350°F/Gas Mark 4.

Cream the butter and sugar until light and fluffy. Beat in the flour and eggs a little at a time, finally beating in the coffee.

Spoon the mixture into two greased and lined 18cm/7in sandwich tins and bake in the centre of the preheated oven for about 25-30 minutes or until well risen and golden. The top should feel firm when lightly pressed.

Turn out carefully onto a wire cooling rack and leave to become cold.

Meanwhile cream the icing sugar and butter together with the coffee until light and creamy. When the coffee cakes are cold, sandwich them together with half of the butter cream and decorate the top with the remainder. Finally decorate the top with the halved walnuts and leave the cake to set before serving.

SPICED CHOCOLATE CAKE

EGYPT

The unusually spicy background of cinnamon and cloves leaps aromatically from both the cake and its cream filling. I found like many cakes from this part of the world, it was truly delectable and ate beautifully, accompanied by a cup of strong dark coffee.

150ml/1/4 pint strong black coffee
150g/5oz dark chocolate
115g/4oz butter
225g/8oz caster sugar
3 medium eggs
225g/8oz self-raising flour
1 level teaspoon cinnamon
1/4 teaspoon ground cloves
1 teaspoon vanilla extract
150ml/1/4 pint milk

Filling/Topping
300ml/1/2 pint double cream
50g/2oz icing sugar
1 teaspoon vanilla extract

A little cinnamon

Preheat the oven to 160°C/325°F/Gas Mark 3. Grease two 18cm/7in sandwich tins, lining the bases with greaseproof paper.

Place the coffee in a small saucepan and add the chocolate, broken into pieces. Place over a low heat, whisking gently to ensure the chocolate is completely melted. Set aside to cool slightly.

In a separate bowl cream the butter and sugar until pale and then add the eggs, flour and spices a little at a time, beating thoroughly with a wooden spoon until completely incorporated. Finally beat in the vanilla, milk and the coffee/chocolate mixture.

Divide the cake mix evenly between the tins and place in a preheated oven to bake for 25-30 minutes or until the cakes spring back when pressed lightly in the centre. Remove from the oven and carefully turn the cakes onto cooling racks and set aside until completely cold.

In a small bowl, whisk the double cream until fairly stiff and then add the icing sugar and vanilla extract. The cream will become stiff enough to stand in peaks.

Place the base of the cake onto a serving plate and spread with half the cream, place the second sponge on top and neatly spoon on the remaining cream, smoothing slightly before sprinkling with a little cinnamon. Refrigerate until required.

RIGO JANCSI / CHOCOLATE SPONGE CAKE

HUNGARY

This marvellous chocolate cake has two seriously chocolatey sponge layers sandwiched together with a dense, wonderfully rich chocolate mousse and an intriguing story behind its name. Rigo Jancsi was a very famous Hungarian gypsy violinist in the early 1900s, playing to devoted listeners at concerts all around Europe. A Belgian duke was in a restaurant with his beautiful young wife, where Rigo Jancsi was playing. The duchess looked at the violinist and was immediately captivated, and she separated from her husband to live with her newfound love, a huge source of scandal and gossip. So this most elaborate of chocolate cakes, was devoted to their passion and named after Rigo Jancsi.

3 large eggs, separated	**Mousse**
75g/3oz caster sugar	115g/4oz dark chocolate
75g/3oz self-raising flour	600ml/1 pint double cream
2 tablespoons cocoa powder	

Preheat the oven to 180°C/350°F/Gas Mark 4.

Whisk the egg yolks and sugar together until pale and creamy. In a separate bowl, whisk the egg whites until stiff.

Slowly whisk the flour and cocoa into the egg yolk and sugar mixture. Finally using a large metal spoon, carefully fold the egg whites into the cake mixture, before spooning the mixture into a greased and lined 20cm/8in cake tin, gently smoothing the top.

Bake the cake in the centre of the preheated oven for about 15-20 minutes or until it feels firm, when pressed gently in the middle.

Turn the cake carefully out onto a wire cooling rack and leave for about 10 minutes before slicing into two rounds. Place one onto a serving plate.

Melt the chocolate in a small bowl over a saucepan of simmering water. Whisk the cream until stiff and removing the chocolate from the saucepan, fold in the melted chocolate.

Spread the mousse over the top of the base sponge and gently place the second sponge on top. Place in the refrigerator to set the mousse.

Before serving dust the top of the cake lightly with icing sugar.

CHOCOLATE RUM CAKE

CARIBBEAN

This densely flavoured cake is utterly delectable, topped with a rich chocolate rum icing. Finished with a choice of Caribbean fruits, which can be peeled, sliced or left whole, depending on how they look the prettiest and laid with an artistic flourish over the cake.

115g/4oz softened butter
115g/4oz muscovado sugar
2 large eggs, lightly beaten
115g/4oz self-raising flour
3 tablespoons sifted cocoa
1/2 teaspoon bicarbonate of soda
1 large banana, mashed
50g/2oz desiccated coconut
1 tablespoon rum

Topping
115g/4oz plain chocolate
3 tablespoons rum
115g/4oz icing sugar
50g/2oz softened butter

Preheat the oven to 180°C/350°F/Gas Mark 4.

Using an electric mixer on high speed, whisk the butter and sugar together until light and fluffy. Using a low speed, whisk in the lightly beaten eggs, self-raising flour, cocoa and bicarbonate of soda. Finally stir in the banana, coconut and rum, ensuring that they are evenly mixed.

Spoon the cake mix into a greased and lightly floured 20cm/8in ring cake tin and smooth the top. Bake in the centre of the preheated oven for about 45 minutes until well risen and springy when pressed lightly. Leave the cake in the tin for about 10 minutes before turning it out onto a cooling rack. I always find it easier to put the rack over the cake before gently turning it over, in order that the cake will drop out of its tin, shaking gently if necessary to release. Ring cakes break fairly easily and removing the cake from its tin in this way helps to avoid the problem.

Meanwhile measure all the topping ingredients into a bowl placed over a saucepan of hot water, stirring with a metal spoon until they have melted and formed a shiny rum icing. Spoon over the top of the cooled cake and allow to drizzle down the outer edge. When set fill the centre of the cake ring with fruits of your choice such as pieces of mango, star fruits etc.

COFFEE AND CHOCOLATE ICE BOX CAKE

USA

A marvellously easy cake to prepare, Ice Box Cakes are not cooked, simply frozen. A lovely cake for a hot summer day teatime or it could possibly be served as a pudding.

275g/10oz plain chocolate
4 tablespoons strong black coffee
275g/10oz softened butter
225g/8oz caster sugar

2 dessertspoons cocoa
4 eggs, separated
275g/10oz digestive biscuits
2 tablespoons rum

Break the chocolate into pieces and put into a small bowl together with the coffee. Place the bowl over a saucepan of simmering water and stir until the chocolate is dissolved. Set aside to cool.

Using a hand mixer, cream the butter and sugar until pale and fluffy. Add the cocoa and whisk to ensure it is well blended.

Whisk in the egg yolks a little at a time. Add the melted chocolate mixture and whisk slowly into the cake mixture.

Finally in a clean bowl, whisk the egg whites until stiff and gently fold them into the cake.

Break the digestive biscuits into pieces and layer half of them into the base of a 23cm/9in loose bottom cake tin lined with greaseproof. Spoon over half of the cake mix, smooth and sprinkle the remaining biscuits over the top. Make another layer with the chocolate cake mix and smooth the top.

Freeze until completely set before serving. Before serving remove from the freezer and place in the fridge to soften slightly, as you would with any ice cream.

DEVIL'S FOOD CAKE

USA

Devil's Food Cake is a rich, chocolate layer cake. It is aptly considered a counterpart to Angel Cake; that is the two cakes are very different: aside from being chocolate-flavoured, the Devil's Cake incorporates butter and far less egg. This cake probably got its name because it was seen as being too tempting to resist.

115g/4oz butter softened
150g/5oz caster sugar
150g/5oz dark muscovado sugar
175g/6oz plain flour
2 tablespoons cocoa powder
1/2 teaspoon bicarbonate of soda
1/2 teaspoon baking powder
2 eggs, lightly beaten
4 tablespoons milk

Topping
50g/2oz softened butter
50g/2oz cocoa powder
350g/12oz sifted icing sugar
5 tablespoons warm water

Preheat the oven to 180°C/350°F/Gas Mark 4. Using an electric hand mixer, cream the butter and sugars together until light and creamy.

Sift the flour, cocoa, bicarbonate of soda and baking powder together and add to the butter mixture, a little at a time, alternating with the eggs and milk.

Ensure the cake mixture is completely combined before spooning half of the cake mix into each of two 18cm/7in sandwich tins, greased and lined with a greaseproof circle. Smooth the tops of the cakes and place them into the centre of the preheated oven.

Bake for about 25 minutes or until well risen and the top of the cakes feel firm to touch.

Leave to cool for a few minutes before carefully turning out onto a cooling rack.

Measure the dry topping ingredients into a small bowl and add the water. Mixing with a hand held electric mixer on a low speed, the mixture should be very soft and of a spreading consistency.

Place the cake onto a serving plate, sandwich the two cakes together with a third of the icing. Spread the remaining mixture over the cake and move to a cool place to set.

Best eaten the following day, to allow the flavour to develop.

APPLE, ORANGE AND LEMON CAKES

The village of Woolsthorpe-by-Colsterworth in Lincolnshire is only a couple of miles away from where I live. It was here in 1666, while resting in his orchard, that Sir Isaac Newton watched an apple fall from a tree, he thus concluded that objects always fall down – never up, and so gave rise to his theory of gravity.

Apples not only gave Isaac Newton his inspiration, they have proved to be a culinary inspiration throughout the centuries; the wonderful apple brandy, Calvados, tastes so very good in cakes and because apples often quickly become mushy, one of the best ways to use them up is to bake with them. German Apple Cake, Apfel Kuchen and the Pennsylvanian Dutch Apple Cake are perfect examples.

Oranges and lemons have always been the most wonderful ingredient for cakes, be it simply an orange or lemon cake flavoured with zest, which is incredibly aromatic, or perhaps using the juice to make a delicious citrus icing or filling.

When looking through the recipes in this section, which include citrus fruits, I noticed how varied they were. Portuguese Polenta Cake, Greek Vasilopita Cake and Tunisian Citrus Cake, my own personal favourite, are all completely different from each other but all with a wonderful tang. How very fortunate are those people who have citrus trees growing in their garden, being able to walk out and pick a piece of fresh fruit and roll it in their hands to release the perfume – it would make me want to rush indoors to bake one of the many cake recipes which follow.

ORANGE AND ALMOND CAKE

SPAIN

This cake is a wonderful example of cooks using ingredients which are near at hand, since both oranges and almonds are so prolific in Spain. Exceptionally delicious, very moist and aromatic, I just know that it will quickly become a firm favourite as it really is difficult to stop at one slice.

6 large eggs, separated
250g/9oz caster sugar
250g/9oz ground almonds
Zest of 1 lemon and 2 oranges

Syrup
Juice of 1 lemon and 4 oranges
115g/4oz caster sugar

Grease and line a 20cm/8in loose base cake tin. Preheat the oven to 180°C/350°F/Gas Mark 4.

In a large bowl, using an electric whisk, whisk the egg whites until stiff. In a separate bowl whisk the egg yolks with the caster sugar until pale and thick. Stir in the ground almonds and zest of lemon and orange before finally folding in the egg whites. Spoon the batter into the cake tin, smoothing lightly and bake in the preheated oven for about an hour until golden brown and firm when pressed lightly in the centre.

Meanwhile put the juice and sugar into a small saucepan and bring to the boil, then lowering the heat, allow the syrup to simmer for 10 minutes. Allow to cool.

Finally, when cooled place the sponge onto a plate, gently peeling off the greaseproof paper before piercing the top several times and gently pouring the orange and lemon syrup over the cake. It is now ready to eat – resist if you can!

TORTA DI LIMONE E MANDORLE / LEMON AND ALMOND CAKE

ITALY

So often I find that Italian cakes are based around nuts, this one is no exception; the ground almonds giving it a wonderful texture and the lemon juice and zest add zing.

150g/5oz softened butter	1 teaspoon baking powder
150g/5oz soft pale brown sugar	Zest and juice of 1 lemon
3 large eggs, separated	
150g/5oz ground almonds	Icing sugar to dust
75g/3oz plain flour	

Preheat the oven to 180°C/350°F/Gas Mark 4. Grease and line an 20cm/8in cake tin.

Cream the butter and sugar until light and fluffy. Beat the egg yolks, flour and baking powder into the mixture a little at a time, finally adding the ground almonds and lemon.

In a small bowl whisk the egg whites until stiff and using a large metal spoon, fold them lightly into the cake mixture.

Spoon the cake mix into your prepared tin and place in the centre of the oven, baking for about 35 minutes or until firm when pressed gently in the centre.

When cooked, allow to cool for 10-15 minutes before gently turning out onto a wire rack. The cake may be eaten slightly warm or cold but either way it is nice lightly dusted with icing sugar.

HUISH CAKE

WALES

Huish Cake, made with ground rice, remains popular in Wales. The root meaning of the word Huish, seems to be 'household' or 'family farm'. It has been suggested that Huishes are survivals of an older, perhaps pre-Saxon, farmstead-based settlement pattern. So perhaps the cake is simply a farmhouse cake. A popular alternative recipe was to add a little caraway seed, just before baking. I recently read that originally it had been served as a baby's christening cake, but I have been unsuccessful in confirming this. This version is flavoured with lemon zest instead.

115g/4oz butter	175g/6oz self-raising flour
175g/6oz caster sugar	115g/4oz ground rice
Zest of 1 large lemon	2 tablespoons milk
4 egg yolks	

Preheat the oven to 180°C/350°F/Gas Mark 4.

Grease and line a 15cm/6in cake tin.

Cream the butter and sugar until pale and fluffy, adding the lemon zest. Beat in the egg yolks, one at a time, adding a little flour if they start to curdle.

Stir in the remaining flour and ground rice, together with the milk.

Spoon the cake mixture into the prepared cake tin and bake in the preheated oven for about 50 to 60 minutes or until it is well risen, golden brown and a skewer inserted into the centre comes out cleanly.

Remove from the oven and allow to cool in the tin for 20 minutes before turning carefully onto a wire cooling rack.

ORANGE AND LEMON POLENTA CAKE

PORTUGAL

Polenta (cornmeal) is incredibly versatile; it can be cooked like porridge, poured into a dish and sliced when cold. Buttered or fried it is a firm favourite in the Mediterranean served with savoury dishes. The ground meal, either coarse or fine, bakes wonderfully into sweet or savoury breads using fruits, sugar, cheese or olives.

The ground almonds and polenta give the cake a slightly coarse texture and a rather crisp top, making it very good to eat and a little different. Incidentally, you can use all lemon or all orange juice and zest according to your preference. Well worth baking.

225g/8oz caster sugar	50g/2oz ground almonds
225g/8oz butter	1 teaspoon baking powder
4 large eggs, lightly beaten	Juice and zest of 1 lemon
115g/4oz self-raising flour	Juice and zest of 1 orange
50g/2oz coarse polenta	

Preheat the oven to 160°C/325°F/Gas Mark 3. Grease and line a 20cm/8in round cake tin.

Place the sugar and butter into a large bowl and using a hand mixer, whisk until pale and creamy. Using the mixer, slowly whisk in the lightly beaten eggs, flour, polenta, ground almonds and baking powder, adding a little at a time to prevent curdling. Add the zest of the lemon and orange and finally, stir in half of the lemon and orange juice.

Spoon the cake mix into the tin and place in the centre of the oven. After 30 minutes press the top of the cake lightly and if it feels firm run a skewer into the centre, if it comes out cleanly the cake is cooked. However, if the cake is still soft, return it to the oven and check every 10 minutes until cooked.

When the cake is cooked, leaving it in its tin, gently pour the remainder of the lemon and orange juice over the top of the cake and allow it to cool before removing from the tin.

APFEL KUCHEN / APPLE CAKE

GERMANY

A truly delectable cake which is wonderfully aromatic, and the way in which it is put together all helps to make it far from ordinary. A layer of cake mixture, a layer of spiced apples and another layer of cake mix, baked to a glorious golden brown, dusted lightly with icing sugar and served with cream. I challenge you to find a more scrummy cake for afternoon tea.

115g/4oz butter
115g/4oz caster sugar
225g/8oz self-raising flour
1 egg, beaten

Filling
450g/1lb Bramley cooking apples
115g/4oz golden sultanas
75g/3oz soft pale brown sugar
Grated zest of a lemon
A little ground cinnamon

Icing sugar

Preheat the oven to 190°C/375°F/Gas Mark 5. Grease and line a 20cm/8in cake tin with baking paper.

Melt the butter and caster sugar in a medium saucepan, stirring until the sugar has dissolved.

Taking the pan from the heat, stir in the flour and egg, beating with a wooden spoon until a soft dough is formed. Divide the dough in half placing one in the cake tin, pressing it to cover the entire bottom of the tin.

Peel and core the apples cutting them into thin slices. Layer the apple slices over the cake mix and sprinkle over the sultanas, sugar, lemon zest and a little cinnamon to taste. Finally, gently press the other half of the cake mixture over the apples, levelling the top as much as possible.

Place in the centre of the preheated oven and cook for about 45 minutes or until it is golden brown. Allow the cake to cool in the tin. It may be eaten hot or cold according to your preference.

CITRUS CAKE

TUNISIA

This is an astonishingly aromatic cake, which I first encountered, while watching Nigella Lawson bake one on TV. The idea of poaching a whole orange until soft, removing the pips, puréeing and then pouring into the creamed cake mix, seemed so unlikely but to my delight worked wonderfully well; the cake is moist but not soggy.

Recently while holidaying in southern Ireland, I saw the brilliant Irish cook, Darina Allen bake a very similar cake with great success, saying she had seen Sophie Grigson bake it. Then when I opened a new cookery book by Diana Henry and read a recipe for a Middle Eastern Citrus Cake, which she said she had originally seen Sophie Grigson bake, I knew with praise from all these well-known cooks, I just had to include what was clearly a really luscious Tunisian delight.

2 medium oranges	**Optional orange butter cream topping**
175g/6oz unsalted butter	175g/6oz butter
175g/6oz caster sugar	175g/6oz icing sugar
3 large eggs, lightly beaten	1 tablespoon fresh orange juice
175g/6oz ground almonds	
50g/2oz breadcrumbs	
1/2 teaspoon mace	

Place the oranges into a small-lidded saucepan, cover them with water. Gently bring to the boil and then simmer for 1 1/2 hours or until soft. Set aside to cool before cutting into four, removing any pips and placing into a food processor, to whiz to a purée.

Preheat the oven to 180°C/350°F/Gas Mark 4. Grease and line a 20cm/8in cake tin.

Cream the butter and sugar until fluffy, add the lightly beaten eggs, ground almonds, breadcrumbs and mace, stirring until fully incorporated. Finally stir in the orange purée.

Spoon into the cake tin, smoothing lightly before baking in the centre of the preheated oven for about 45 minutes, or until the cake feels just firm when lightly pressed in the centre. It is important to remember that this is a very moist cake and it will remain sticky even when cooked.

If liked an orange butter cream icing may be smoothed over the top of the cake when cold; personally I think this makes the cake irresistible.

VASILOPITA CAKE

GREECE

This Greek New Year cake is dedicated to St Basil, Patron Saint of wishes and blessings. Traditionally a coin is added to the mixture, and whoever gets it will have good luck for the year. The entire cake is cut into the number of pieces needed to serve each guest, and the cake is served in a particular order, from oldest to youngest. And, in fact, everyone who eats this lovely nut cake will have good luck because it is so moist and delicious.

150g/5oz butter
275g/10oz caster sugar
1 teaspoon finely grated orange rind
1 teaspoon finely grated lemon rind
3 lightly beaten eggs
225g/8oz self-raising flour
125ml/4fl oz milk
1 dessertspoon orange juice

1 dessertspoon lemon juice
3 tablespoons chopped pecan nuts
3 tablespoons flaked almonds

Topping
6 tablespoons nuts of your choice
Pecans/almonds/pistachios/walnuts

Preheat the oven to 160°C/325°F/Gas Mark 3. Grease and line a 20cm/8in cake tin.

Cream the butter and sugar until pale and fluffy, adding the orange and lemon rind before stirring in the eggs and flour, a little of each at a time. Add the orange and lemon juice, together with the remaining milk, finally stirring in the pecan nuts and almonds.

Spoon the cake mixture into the prepared tin, lightly smoothing the top and sprinkling with your choice of nuts.

Bake in the centre of the oven for about 1 1/2 hours, covering the cake with a sheet of brown paper if it begins to brown before it is cooked through. When firm to touch remove the cake from the oven and allow to cool for about 15 minutes before turning it onto a wire rack.

ORANGE AND CHOCOLATE CAKE

NEW ZEALAND

The amazingly good texture of this cake is a direct result of the ground almonds, which take the place of flour. Very popular in New Zealand, it takes a little extra time and effort to make, but is well worthwhile as it is really delicious.

1 whole orange
120g/4oz caster sugar
225g/8oz plain chocolate, melted
120g/4oz ground almonds
3 large eggs, separated
1/2 teaspoon baking powder

Topping
A little icing sugar

Place the orange into a small saucepan adding 300ml/1/2 pint water and simmer turning occasionally, until it is soft. Set aside to cool in the covered bowl. When the orange is cold, preheat the oven to 190°C/375°F/Gas Mark 5 and grease and line a 20cm/8 inch spring form cake tin.

Cut the orange into quarters, removing the pips and whiz in a food processor with 4 tablespoons of the orange liquid in which the orange was cooked. Add the sugar, melted chocolate, ground almonds, egg yolks and baking powder, processing just enough to mix all the ingredients together. Pour the almond mixture into a large bowl. Beat the egg whites until stiff and using a metal spoon, fold them into the cake mix using a figure of 8 movement.

Pour the mixture into the cake tin, place it into the centre of the preheated oven and cook for 30 minutes before gently opening the oven door and covering the cake with a sheet of baking paper. Continue baking for a further 30 minutes or until the cake feels firm to touch.

Remove the baked cake from the oven and allow it to become completely cold before removing it carefully from the tin and placing on a plate. If liked sprinkle with a little icing sugar before serving.

PENNSYLVANIAN DUTCH APPLE CAKE

USA

When the Dutch settled in America, one of the legacies they brought with them which are still used today, are some wonderful food recipes. The Pennsylvanian Dutch Apple Cake is one of the most famous cake recipes.

5 medium apples, peeled and sliced	300ml/1/2 pint vegetable oil
50g/2oz caster sugar	2 teaspoons vanilla extract
2 teaspoons ground cinnamon	2 tablespoons lemon juice
350g/12oz plain flour	1 teaspoon bicarbonate of soda
350g/12oz soft pale brown sugar	1 teaspoon baking powder
4 large eggs	Icing sugar

Preheat the oven to 180°C/350°F/Gas Mark 4. Grease and flour a 23cm/9in round cake tin.

Coat the apple slices in the caster sugar and ground cinnamon.

In a large bowl using an electric hand held mixer, mix together the flour, sugar, eggs, oil, vanilla, lemon juice, soda and baking powder, ensuring the mixture is lump free.

Spoon a third of the cake mixture into the prepared cake tin and arrange half of the apple slices on the top. Repeat using all the apples and finishing with a final layer of the cake mixture.

Bake in the centre of the oven for about 1 hour until the cake feels firm to touch. Allow the cake to cool completely before removing it from its tin, placing on a plate and dusting with a little sifted icing sugar.

CARDAMOM CREAM CAKE

PAKISTAN

So many Pakistani cakes closely resemble Indian sweetmeats, sticky, aromatic and truly delectable that it is easy to see which ingredients are prolific in this part of the world.

The Cardamom Cream Cake, enhanced by orange juice and zest, is really more like a heavily scented sponge, which may be topped with freshly whipped cream.

150g/5oz softened butter
250g/9oz caster sugar
115g/4oz fresh cream
250g/9oz sifted plain flour
1 1/2 teaspoons of baking powder
4 large eggs, separated

1/2 teaspoon orange zest
1/4 teaspoon ground cardamom
1/4 teaspoon ground mace
75ml/3fl oz fresh orange juice

Extra Cream for topping

Preheat the oven to 180°C/350°F/Gas Mark 4. Grease and line, with greaseproof paper, an 18cm/7in round cake tin.

Measure the butter, sugar and cream into a bowl and using an electric hand mixer, cream together until pale and fluffy.

Whisking on a low speed, add the flour, baking powder, and egg yolks a little at a time until well blended and then add the orange zest, cardamom, mace and orange juice continuing to whisk gently.

In a separate bowl, whisk the egg whites until stiff and using a large metal spoon gently fold them into the cake mixture.

Finally, pour the batter into the greased and lined cake tin and place in the centre of the preheated oven to cook. After about 30 minutes, look at the cake and check that when pressed lightly in the centre it feels springy to touch, if not put back into the oven and check after another 10 minutes or until a skewer inserted into the centre comes out cleanly.

Allow to cool in the tin for 10 minutes before gently turning out onto a wire cooling rack and leave to become completely cold before removing the greaseproof paper.

If liked you may whisk some double cream to spread over the top of the cake.

LEMON CHIFFON CAKE

USA

Not unlike an Angel Cake in texture, the use of vegetable oil instead of butter together with the high proportion of eggs, gives a moist texture and a wonderfully delicate flavour.

The zest and juice of lemon gives the cake an extra zing, but a favourite variation is to add cocoa and grated chocolate – delicious.

225g/8oz self-raising flour
275g/10oz caster sugar
1 tablespoon baking powder
125ml/4fl oz vegetable oil
6 large eggs, separated
Zest and juice of 4 large lemons

Lemon icing
225g/8oz icing sugar
Juice of 1 lemon

Preheat the oven to 160°C/325°F/Gas Mark 3. Grease and flour a 23cm/9in ring cake tin.

Sift together the flour, sugar and baking powder into a large bowl.

Using an electric hand mixer slowly beat in the vegetable oil, egg yolks, zest and juice of the lemons, ensuring that the mixture is lump free.

In a clean bowl, whisk the egg whites with the hand mixer, using clean beaters, until stiff and with a large metal spoon gently fold them into the cake mixture.

Pour the batter into the prepared cake tin and bake in the preheated oven for about 1 hour, or until a skewer inserted into the centre comes out cleanly.

Remove the cake from the oven and placing a wire cake rack over the top of the cake, turn it upside down and shake gently to release it. Allow the cake to become completely cold.

Meanwhile prepare the lemon icing by mixing the icing sugar and lemon juice together, to form a thin glaze. You may add a little more icing sugar if necessary to give the right consistency.

Gently drizzle the icing over the cake, allowing it to run down the sides.

TORTA DI POLENTA MANDORLE E LIMONE / LEMON AND ALMOND POLENTA CAKE

ITALY

Polenta has been part of the staple diet of northern Italy for centuries. Ground from maize, polenta comes in many grades from very fine through to coarse, but generally speaking, finely ground is best for cakes. This particular recipe also contains ricotta, the wonderfully soft, aromatic, sheep cheese, which is greatly enhanced by the lemon zest and juice and ground almonds. Simple to make, the pine nuts and golden sultanas are optional extras but well worth including.

150g/5oz softened butter	Juice of 1 lemon
115g/4oz ricotta cheese	1/2 teaspoon vanilla extract
225g/8oz caster sugar	115g/4oz finely ground polenta
225g/8oz ground almonds	1 teaspoon baking powder
3 large eggs	50g/2oz pine nuts
Zest of two lemons	50g/2oz golden sultanas

Preheat the oven to 160°C/325°F/Gas Mark 3. Grease and lightly flour a 18cm/7in spring release cake tin.

Cream the butter, ricotta cheese and caster sugar together until pale and fluffy.

Beat in the ground almonds and eggs, a little at a time.

Stir in the lemon zest and juice, the vanilla extract, polenta and baking powder.

Finally if liked, stir in the pine nuts and golden sultanas.

Spoon into the prepared cake tin, lightly smoothing the top, before placing in the centre of the preheated oven.

Bake for approximately 30-40 minutes or until the cake feels 'set' when pressed gently in the centre.

Allow to cool completely in the tin, before releasing the spring and transferring the cake onto a plate. Dust lightly with sifted icing sugar before serving.

APPLE STREUSEL CAKE

GERMANY

This wonderfully aromatic cake is really very simple to make. It is the addition of a layer of apples, together with a cinnamon topping, which makes it so special. The streusel topping made with dark muscovado sugar, has a depth of colour, which clearly contrasts with the pale cake and apples underneath.

2 large cooking apples, sliced and lightly
  poached
225g/8oz caster sugar
225g/8oz softened butter
3 large eggs
350g/12oz self-raising flour
150ml/¼ pint milk

Streusel topping
115g/4oz flour
115g/4oz dark brown sugar
4 level teaspoons cinnamon
75g/3oz butter from refrigerator

Preheat the oven to 180°C/350°F/Gas Mark 4. Grease and line a 23cm/9in square cake tin.

In a small bowl, using an electric hand mixer, beat the butter and sugar together until pale and fluffy. Add the eggs, beating slowly.

On the lowest speed, add the flour and milk a little at a time. Spoon just over half of the cake mixture into the baking tin and smooth the top. Place the apple slices in neat rows before topping with the remaining cake mixture and smoothing the top.

Using a pallet knife, stir the flour, sugar and cinnamon together in a small bowl and taking the butter from the refrigerator, grate it into the streusel topping and stir gently with the pallet knife to distribute it evenly.

Sprinkle the topping over the cake and place into the centre of the preheated oven, to bake for about an hour or until the cake feels firm to touch.

Leave the cake in its tin to become completely cold, before lifting out and peeling away the greaseproof paper then cutting into equally sized square portions.

INDEX

CAKES BY COUNTRY

INDEX

SOURCES and BIBLIOGRAPHY

With thanks to: Kate Hart, Sally Baxter, Anna McNamee, Dr Sheena Bradley, Pamela Bradshaw, Kenneth and Ruth Wallace, Thelma Weston, Elsie Bristow, Andrew Blinman, Belinda Duff, Jenny Davies, Pippa Lord, Foster & Jackie Edwards, Llynne Sikorski, Geoff Lewin, Aurora Luna, Joshua Allen, Sheila Morris and to all the friends who came up with recipes from their homelands and holiday visits.

Research and reading material: Aris, Fleetwood, Bacon *Food and Cooking of Spain, Africa and the Middle East,* Lorenz 2006; Bacon and Fleetwood *Middle Eastern Cookery,* Hermes House 2006; Boswell *Great Cakes and Pies,* USA; Brazier, Marie *Gateaux de Mamie,* Marabout 2002; Chamberlain, Lesley *The Best of Eastern Europe,* Hermes House 2003; *Cooking Moroccan,* Murdoch Books 2005; David, Elizabeth *English Bread and Yeast Cookery,* Penguin 2001; Day, Martha *Baking,* Lorenz 2003; *Favourite Recipes from Famous New Orleans,* Colour Picture Publishers, USA 1981; *Food of Italy* Murdoch Books 2006; Halverhout, Heleen *Dutch Cooking* De Driehoek 1961; Husain, Shehzad *Indian Cooking* London 1998; Jerome, Helen *Concerning Cake Making* Pitman 1932; Koichiro, Hata *Practical Japanese Cooking,* Kodansha 1997; Koval, Romana *Jewish Cooking,* London 2001; Lapp, Sally *Amish Cooking: Specialties of Lancaster County*; Mallos, Tess *The Complete Middle East Cookbook,* Grub Street 1995; Markham, Gervaise *The English Huswife,* London 1615; Ojakangas, Beatrice *Scandinavian Baking Book* University of Minnesota Press 1999; Ojakangas, Beatrice *Scandinavian Feasts,* Stewart, Tabori & Chang USA 1992; *Sister Jennie's Shaker Desserts* Gabriel's Horn Publishing Co. USA 1983.

TEMPLATE FOR GINGERBREAD HOUSE (page 152)

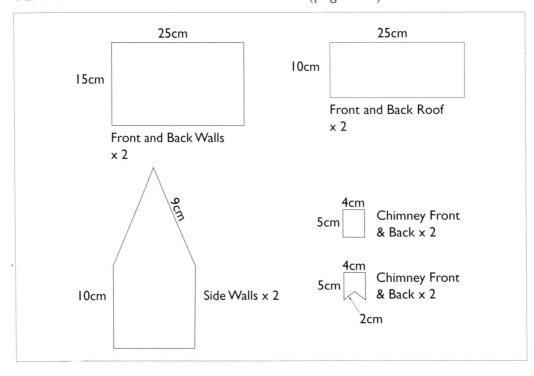